Supporting Content Area Literacy with Technology

William G. Brozo
George Mason University

Kathleen S. Puckett
Arizona State University

Boston   New York   San Francisco
Mexico City   Montreal   Toronto   London   Madrid   Munich   Paris
Hong Kong   Singapore   Tokyo   Cape Town   Sydney

Executive Editor: Aurora Martínez Ramos
Series Editorial Assistant: Kara Kikel
Executive Marketing Manager: Krista Clark
Marketing Manager: Danae April
Production Editor: Paula Carroll
Editorial Production Service: Lynda Griffiths
Composition Buyer: Linda Cox
Manufacturing Buyer: Megan Cochran
Electronic Composition: Schneck-DePippo Graphics
Cover Administrator: Linda Knowles

For Professional Development resources visit www.allynbaconmerrill.com.

Between the time website information is gathered and then published, it is not unusual for some sites to have closed. Also, the transcription of URLs can result in typographical errors. The publisher would appreciate notification where these errors occur so that they may be corrected in subsequent editions.

Cataloging-in-Publication data unavailable at press time.

Printed in the United States of America

10 9 8 7 6 5 4 3 2 1   12 11 10 09 08

**Allyn & Bacon
is an imprint of**

ISBN-10:   0-205-51185-6
ISBN-13: 978-0-205-51185-3

Contents

Preface

Supporting Content Area Literacy with Technology is the only book of its kind available to teachers today. It brings together the most current research and practice in reading and writing with instructional technology in a unique practical guide for improving the literacy skills and content knowledge of students from kindergarten through the middle grades. The need for such a book couldn't be greater in light of the ever-increasing demands placed on students to develop high levels of academic literacy in order to access additional educational opportunities and to become engaged citizens in the information age.

The single-most important tool children and youth need to become effective problem solvers, flexible decision makers, and critical thinkers is *skillful reading ability*. Skilled readers are far more likely to be successful at home and in the workplace than their unskilled peers. Sadly, too many children in the elementary years are failing to develop adequate skills and strategies for comprehending academic text and communicating effectively using academic language. These students are at risk of entering middle and high school with literacy levels too low to ensure success in content classrooms. Not surprising, it is estimated that every day between 3,000 and 7,000 students drop out of American schools (Alliance for Excellent Education, 2007; Kids Count, 2004). Dropouts are often doomed to grinding cycles of poverty, unemployment, and other economic, social, and personal setbacks (Center for Workforce Preparation, 2004; Sum, 2007). In a world driven by information and knowledge, their skill deficiencies will limit access to the full range of opportunities enjoyed by their more literate peers (Hofstetter, Sticht, & Hofstetter, 1999). Thus, the quality of literacy competence individuals develop as children and youth will impact their competence in personal, occupational, and community life as adults (Brozo & Simpson, 2007).

For the past 30 years a consistent pattern has emerged from National Assessment of Educational Progress data. Although most elementary and middle students can read and comprehend text at basic levels, fewer have demonstrated competencies on more challenging comprehension tasks (Donahue, Daane, & Grigg, 2003). Furthermore, in the most recent national assessment, nearly 36 percent of fourth-graders and 26 percent of eighth-graders were considered to be struggling readers (Perie, Grigg, & Donahue, 2005). Confirming this pattern are data from *The Nation's Report Card: U.S. History 2001* (Lapp, Grigg, & Tay-Lim, 2002) indicating that over 80 percent of elementary and middle school students were below the proficient level in comprehension. Overrepresented in this category are children of color and those from lower-income levels (Perie, Grigg, & Donahue, 2005).

Meeting the challenge of developing competent readers of academic text is why *Supporting Content Area Literacy with Technology* was developed. And it does so by demonstrating how engaging, evidence-based literacy strategies can be offered to students in the elementary and middle grades using accessible, teacher-friendly technology tools.

Taking advantage of technology to mediate content literacy strategies is an approach, we argue, whose time has come and makes sense in today's digital age. The strongest advocates for the use of technology tools in teaching and learning claim its most appealing feature is that students are automatically interested in and motivated by computers, and that this high level of enthusiasm will give rise to higher academic achievement (Leu, Kinzer, Coiro, & Cammack, 2004). Indeed, there is growing evidence to support the motivating effects of computers when used with students in school-based learning (Rozell & Gardner, 2000; Sølvberg, 2003). If students are more enthusiastic about learning with technology tools, then these tools should be exploited to whatever extent they can to build literacy skills and bring about meaningful and critical exploration of content.

Overview

Supporting Content Area Literacy with Technology is a resource designed to help K–8 teachers improve students' acquisition of effective *academic literacy skills* and *content knowledge*. It is built on a firm foundation of evidence and incorporates elements and strategies that are recommended by expert panels and in reports such as *Reading for Understanding* (Snow, 2002), *Reading Next* (Biancarosa & Snow, 2004), and *Writing Next* (Graham & Perin, 2007).

To make content area learning more engaging and meaningful for all students, we present teachers with a basic framework for pairing literacy strategies with readily available classroom technology. Drawing on concepts of universal design and flexible curriculum access, we demonstrate how content literacy strategies can be given technology applications to make them more engaging and responsive to the learning needs of all students. We also explore legislation authorizing the use of technology for learners with diverse abilities and offer teachers tools to make technology work in their classrooms for these learners. Our evidence-based practices, explicit instructional strategies, and authentic activities guide teachers in integrating curriculum with English/language arts, social studies, science, and math to reduce the barriers to learning and improve student achievement. *Supporting Content Area Literacy with Technology* is written in a teacher-friendly voice with advice and suggestions for helping teachers make technology adaptations to turn their classrooms into powerful learning communities that foster reading comprehension and content learning for all students.

Chapter Organization

This book fills an important need for classroom teachers who are seeking ways to make learning of content material in English/language arts, social studies, science, and math more engaging and meaningful to students across the ability spectrum. Evidence abounds that teachers throughout the United States lack appropriate training and skills in teaching literacy strategies. Despite great efforts at infrastructure development, technology use in the K–12 curriculum lags behind home, personal, and business uses. Furthermore, recent research has shown that technology is a powerful tool for helping readers who struggle with literacy skills, by providing students with the means for accessing literacy supports independently, within the curriculum task, and at the moment needed. Technology provides teachers with the ability to manage supports for students with a wide variety of abilities, allowing more concentration on the content of the learning standard at hand.

Supporting Content Area Literacy with Technology shows teachers how to harness the power of pairing technology with literacy strategies to support content learning for all students. This book demonstrates how to use technology, not as a separate entity but as a tool for providing literacy strategy supports. To that end, Chapter 1 begins with an overview of the approach taken in this book, defines content literacy, and provides a rationale for using technology to mediate literacy strategies for content learning for the diverse population of students in elementary and middle school classrooms today. Chapter 2 provides a research rationale and instructional framework for 11 evidence-based content literacy strategies that reappear in subsequent chapters paired with technology tools. These strategies are thoroughly explained and exemplified in this chapter. Next, Chapter 3 demonstrates the value of using a Universal Design for Learning (UDL) framework for identifying appropriate technology tools that are responsive to the needs of diverse students and are a compliment to the content literacy strategies. In Chapters 4 through 7 the content literacy strategies with technology applications are exemplified in extended classroom vignettes from English/language arts, science, social studies, and math. The book concludes with Chapter 8, which reviews the various technology tools found in the preceding chapters. Insights and little-known features of these tools useful to the classroom teacher are described and vendor information is shared.

Special Features

Supporting Content Area Literacy with Technology takes a unique approach and contains many special features that make the book a useful guide to K–8 teachers interested in using accessible technology tools to teach effective literacy strategies and increase students' content learning. The following list highlights these important features:

- Demonstrates how instructional technology can become the medium for teaching and learning literacy strategies in all subject areas

- Helps teachers to plan flexible strategies to meet a wide range of student abilities with explicit instruction examples

- Guides teachers in developing skills in both content area teaching and effective use of instructional and assistive technology

- Provides teachers of subject areas tools for meeting the content learning needs of all students

- Focuses attention on the importance of helping all students, including those with disabilities, meet content standards

- Takes advantage of the interactive nature of instructional technology for motivating students to become more engaged and thoughtful learners

- Includes "Think and Apply" feature that prompts readers to reflect on ideas and strategies gleaned from the chapter content and to consider innovative ways of applying this new knowledge in instructional contexts

- Features "Questions for Study" to aid facilitators in further discussion and learning in book club study groups

- Presents classroom examples of content literacy and technology within a content area (social studies, English/language arts, science, and math), including content standards, sample text, application of content strategies for readiness, interactive comprehension, and extending new learning

References

Alliance for Excellent Education. (2007, January). *The high cost of high school dropouts: What the nation pays for inadequate high schools.* Washington, DC: Author.

Biancarosa, G., & Snow, C. (2004). *Reading next: A vision for action and research in middle and high school literacy.* New York/Washington, DC: Carnegie Corporation/Alliance for Excellent Education.

Brozo, W. G., & Simpson, M. L. (2007). *Content literacy for today's adolescents: Honoring diversity and building competence.* Upper Saddle River, NJ: Merrill/Prentice-Hall.

Center for Workforce Preparation. (2004). *A chamber guide to improving workplace literacy.* Washington, DC: U.S. Chamber of Commerce.

Donahue, P., Daane, M., & Grigg, W. (2003). *The nation's report card: Reading highlights 2003.* Washington, DC: National Center for Education Statistics.

Graham, S., & Perin, D. (2007). *Writing next: Effective strategies to improve writing of adolescents in middle and high schools.* New York: Carnegie Corporation.

Hofstetter, C., Sticht, T., & Hofstetter, C. (1999). Knowledge, literacy and power. *Communication Research, 26*, 58–80.

Kids Count. (2004). *Kids Count 2004 data book online.* www.aecf.org/cgi-bin/kc.cgi?action=profile&area=United+States.

Lapp, M., Grigg, W. S., & Tay-Lim, B. (2002). *The nation's report card: U.S. history 2001* (National Center for Education Statistics Publication

No. NCES-2002-483). Washington, DC: U.S. Department of
Education, Education Publications Center.

Leu, D. J., Kinzer, C. K., Coiro, J. L., & Cammack, D. W. (2004). Toward
a theory of new literacies emerging from the Internet and other
information and communication technologies. In R. Ruddell & N.
Unrau (Eds.), *Theoretical models and processes of reading* (5th ed.).
Newark, DE: International Reading Association.

Perie, M., Grigg, W., & Donahue, P. (2005). *The nation's report card:
Reading 2005* (National Center for Education Statistics Publication
No. NCES 2006–451). Washington, DC: U.S. Department of
Education, U.S. Government Printing Office.

Rozell, E. J., & Gardner, W. L. (2000). Cognitive, motivation, and affective processes associated with computer related performance: A
path analysis. *Computers in Human Behavior, 16,* 199–222.

Snow, C. (2002). *Reading for understanding: Toward an R&D program in reading comprehension.* Santa Monica, CA: Rand Education.

Sølvberg, A. (2003). Computer-related control beliefs and motivation:
A panel study. *Journal of Research on Technology in Education, 35,*
473–487.

Sum, A. (2007, March). *The educational attainment of the nation's young
black men and their recent labor market experiences: What can be done
to improve their future labor market and educational prospects.* Boston:
Center for Labor Market Studies, Northeastern University.

Acknowledgments

This preface would be incomplete without recognizing the supporting role of Allyn & Bacon editorial and production staff. A very special thanks to Aurora Martínez, our editor and friend, whose vision and commitment turned an interesting idea in our minds into this grounded and practical resource for teachers. Thanks as well go out to our production editor Paula Carroll and our production coordinator Lynda Griffiths for their specific assistance in ensuring the book is teacher-friendly both in language and format.

We are, of course, extremely indebted to our diligent reviewers whose helpful insights and suggestions have made this a better book. They are Heidi Davey, Hoffman Estates High School; Vera Faulkner, Consortium of Universities of the Washington Metropolitan Area; Nancy DeVries Guth, Stafford County Public Schools; Elissa Wolfe Poel, New Mexico State University; Donald D. Pottorff, Grand Valley State University; Melodie Santana, Loyola Marymount University; and Patti Taillacq, Marlborough Intermediate Elementary.

We also express our enormous gratitude to all the teachers, students, and colleagues whose experiences with literacy and technology inspired us to write this book.

Finally, we thank Carol, Bill's wife, and Tom, Kathy's husband, for giving us the time, space, and unflagging support we needed to complete this book.

CHAPTER 1

Content Literacy and Technology: A Twenty-First–Century Approach For Children with Diverse Abilities

Seeing Forward

Our elementary schools are as diverse now as at any time in the history of American schooling. With this diversity comes numerous challenges, not the least of which is ensuring all children develop literacy and learning skills to acquire information and concepts in the content areas, such as language arts, social studies, science, and math. In this chapter you will be introduced to a unique approach designed to meet this challenge. The marriage of content literacy with new computer technology is one whose time has come. Children today living in the mediasphere (O'Brien, 2001) are comfortable interacting with computers. Computer technology is motivating and provides visual support for learning. Furthermore, content literacy strategies can be mediated by computer technology in ways that differentiate instruction to meet the reading, writing, and learning needs of students with diverse abilities and backgrounds.

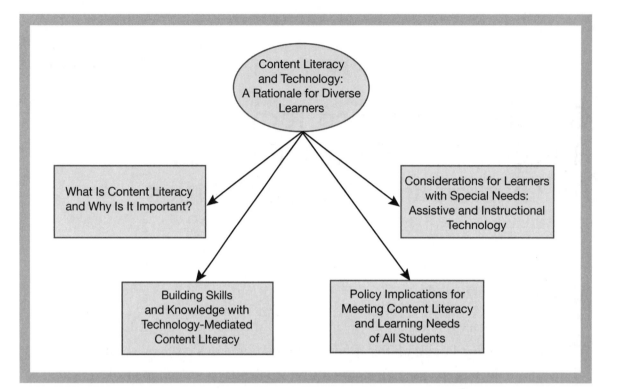

Content Literacy and Technology: A Rationale for Diverse Learners

It is the rare teacher, indeed, who can boast like the denizen of Lake Wobegon that all her students are above average. Most of today's elementary school classrooms are as diverse as ever, with children from a wide spectrum of cultures and a range of socio-economic levels. These children also vary, sometimes quite dramatically, in their ability to read, write, express themselves orally, and learn curricular content. Consequently, meeting the literacy and learning needs of the new diverse student population has become the quintessential challenge of teachers in the twenty-first century.

What Is Content Literacy and Why Is It Important?

3

Content Literacy
and Technology:
A Twenty-First–
Century Approach
for Children with
Diverse Abilities

Content literacy instructional practices are those that braid reading, writing, and thinking with content material from the disciplines, such as language arts, social studies, science, and math. They're premised on the belief that students not only need to learn the content of the curriculum but also ways of reading, writing, and thinking about the content. They teach students independent strategic reading and writing processes for content area learning. Content literacy practices should be modeled and prompted by the teacher and eventually internalized and initiated by students.

Why are content literacy strategies advocated and employed? Chiefly because they help students of all abilities use reading and writing in the service of learning while building independent, strategic reading skills. Another significant goal of content literacy is to help students see that content knowledge and the ability to communicate that knowledge are one in the same. Literacy across the curriculum means students are afforded opportunities to learn and use literacy processes throughout the school day, which has been shown to elevate overall literacy abilities and increase academic achievement (Brozo & Simpson, 2007).

Another reason content literacy is essential for high academic achievement is that with each passing year, the school curriculum places an ever-increasing demand on literacy, as the purpose of reading and writing shifts toward gaining knowledge and expressing new understandings. Because reading problems that may develop in the primary grades tend to become generalized over time, affecting cognitive development and overall performance in all subjects (Stanovich, 1986), it's critical that young children receive instruction that builds literacy skills not just during language arts period but throughout the school day.

Even while content literacy becomes increasingly important as children progress through the grades, the very nature of content area literacy instruction is being regularly redefined through emerging technologies (International Reading Association, 2001). Since literacy can no longer be thought of as only the effective use of paper, pencil, and books, content literacy instruction should not be restricted to traditional oral- and print-based approaches. Diverse students need supportive practices that build proficiencies in locating and reading information from digitized sources, and that scaffold different forms of expression. Not only must students be taught the critical literacy skills needed for effective information use, they must be proficient users of rapidly evolving technology while developing the capacity to use yet unimagined new literacies (International Reading Association, 2001).

Building Skills and Knowledge with Technology-Mediated Content Literacy

One important way of increasing the chances for early academic success for all children and helping them reach their achievement potential is by providing special supports for content learning. All children, regardless of background and ability level, will be introduced to new information, concepts, and vocabulary from topics in language arts, social studies, science, and math. To maximize understanding of this content material and better prepare them for an increasingly sophisticated discipline-based curriculum, children need to develop specialized reading and writing skills and strategies.

Content reading strategies have been around for a long time; however, their application to learning in the early grades has only recently been recognized as a critical component of primary and elementary school curricular standards (Alvermann, Swafford, & Montero, 2004). Texts covering topics in science, social studies, and math are typically written in non-narrative form. Experts agree that to have success reading and comprehending informational, content texts, students—particularly in the early grades—need greater exposure to this type of reading material (Caswell & Duke, 1998; Duke, 2000). The more children encounter content texts, the more they will need effective instruction in content literacy strategies in order to profit from their reading (Duke & Bennett-Armistead, 2003).

Taught in traditional ways, content literacy strategies have been shown to increase engagement, improve reading and writing skills, and expand content knowledge (Fisher & Frey, 2006). These same strategies when mediated by computer technology can become even more engaging and responsive to the unique instructional needs of the children attending our schools today (Puckett & Brozo, 2005).

The most appealing feature of this approach to content teaching and learning is that students are automatically interested in and motivated by computers (Leu, Kinzer, Coiro, & Cammack, 2004). There is a growing body of research to support the motivating effects of computers when used with students in school-based learning (Leu, Kinzer, Coiro, & Cammack, 2004; Rozell & Gardner, 2000; Sølvberg, 2003). If students are more enthusiastic about learning when using digital tools, then teachers of content material should exploit these tools to whatever extent they can to increase children's literacy development and knowledge acquisition.

The use of certain software programs and accompanying hardware for students with diverse abilities has been reported in the technology literature for a number of years (Behrmann & Jerome, 2002; Edyburn, 2000; Kaplan & Edyburn, 1998). Technology options for acquiring content knowledge and literacy skills has become increasingly attractive for teachers and students, as this teaching and learning resource becomes more and more widespread. Indeed, technology tools to expand literacy and content learning are available to virtually every teacher and student. A report of school-based computer technology and Internet access in U.S. public schools (Kleiner & Farris, 2002) found that availability levels have reached nearly 100 percent today. This means that most children, regardless of whether computer technology tools are available in the home, should have access to computers in schools and classrooms. At the same time, at least 31 states require core technical competencies based on national educational standards (Loschert, 2003). These standards serve to further institutionalize the need to weave computer-based teaching and learning into all areas of the school curriculum (Brozo & Simpson, 2007).

Certainly, in spite of the prevalence of computers in school, taking full advantage of their teaching and learning potential in the content areas will depend on elementary teachers' interest and willingness to become more tech savvy (Tileston, 2004). It will also take a commitment from school leaders to make computer programs available and to provide technology supports to teachers (Norris & Soloway, 2003).

Technology may be omnipresent in schools but not everyone is tapping into its educational benefits (Pearson & Young, 2002; Songer, Lee, & Kam, 2002). For instance, in a study of teachers' technology skills (Newman, 2000), only a few of the teachers interviewed had experience with more than email and word-processing programs. Nevertheless, the stretch from email to the vast and learning-rich potential of computer applications in the content areas is much easier than some teachers might think (Richardson, 2004). We acknowledge that what may seem like small changes to us are often big changes for teachers. Thus, we offer helpful guidelines for selecting appropriate technology tools and numerous classroom demonstrations of easy-to-implement, computer-based practices.

One note of caution is needed, however. As the recent Department of Education (DOE) sponsored technology study suggests, when commercially prepared computer software programs comprise the whole of a reading or math curriculum, high student achievement is not guaranteed (National Center for Educational Evaluation, 2007). However, the DOE study also confirmed that teachers who understand the benefits of software and, consequently, use it more effectively, can bring about improved reading performance. What sets the approach we advocate and demonstrate apart from the one-size-fits-all software programs in the DOE study is the role of the teacher in instructional decision making. We believe the teacher's sensitivity to the content literacy and learning needs of her or his students will lead to the judicious use of computer technology tools to meet those needs. The overriding criterion teachers of children should apply when considering the use of computer technology tools in their lessons is the extent to which they will promote engaged reading and learning, and expand children's understanding of information and concepts in the content areas. We and others (Kinzer, 2003; Leu, 2000) believe that teachers who create learning contexts where the importance of critical reading and thinking is valued will find appropriate ways to integrate computer programs and tools in support of content learning.

Policy Implications for Meeting Content Literacy and Learning Needs of All Students

Under the No Child Left Behind Act (NCLB, 2001), schools are now held more accountable than ever before for the progress of all students, including those who present the greatest teaching challenges: students with disabilities, students from poverty, and students who are English learners. Unfortunately, assessment results show that progress toward achieving curriculum standards is still problematic for these students, even while legislation affirms the expectation that they will have access to the general education curriculum in order to meet high academic standards and clear performance goals (Individuals with Disabilities Education Improvement Act of 2004). Making it possible for students of diverse abilities and needs to have maximum opportunities to achieve within the general education curriculum and meet required learning standards, teachers will need to employ more effective and innovative strategies and methods.

The available evidence about children's reading achievement presents a significant challenge to teachers in the primary through intermediate grades. According to the National Assessment of Educational Progress (2002), 36 percent of students were found to have reading proficiency levels below "basic." Problems with reading exhibited in the early grades often remain with children as they progress through elementary, middle, and high school. For instance, Francis and associates (1996) tracked children with reading difficulties from the third grade to the ninth grade and discovered that depressed reading achievement persisted for at least 74 percent of the students. Children who struggle to read are especially vulnerable to failure with content text that demands they possess discipline-specific vocabulary knowledge and sophisticated study reading skills (Alvermann, Swafford, & Montero, 2004; Fisher & Fry, 2006; Puckett & Brozo, 2005).

The growing number of students with disabilities who are included in the general education classroom places further demands on teachers responsible for helping children meet content standards across the curriculum. Estimates vary, but most agree that about 20 percent of all children have some type of reading disability (Shaywitz, 2003). Furthermore, as many as 70 to 80 percent of students with a learning disability also have a reading impairment.

Students in poverty also bring unique needs to the nation's elementary classrooms. Growing up poor places children at risk of academic underachievement (Duncan & Brooks-Dunn, 1997), and family poverty correlates highly with depressed IQ and lower verbal ability (Battistich et al., 1995). On the bright side, an important finding gleaned from analysis of data from large literacy assessments (e.g., Program for International Student Assessment; Progress in International Reading Literacy Study) is that children from low socioeconomic groups who have high engagement in reading also have higher reading achievement than might otherwise be predicted. This is heartening news, because it suggests that income alone does not foretell the educational potential of students. Nevertheless, children of poverty without appropriate instructional supports to boost motivation and reading skill have been shown to compare far less favorably with their more economically privileged peers (Berliner, 2006; Duncan & Seymour, 2000).

Finally, an unparalleled level of transnational migration has meant ever-growing numbers of students with limited English skills entering the nation's elementary schools. The United States Department of Education estimates over 5 million school-aged children in this category, two times the number of just one decade ago (Hawkins, 2004). Teachers responsible for teaching subject-area content are confronted with special challenges trying to meet the literacy and learning needs of increasing numbers of these language-diverse students.

In spite of the challenges, meeting the reading and learning needs of diverse students is no longer an option but a legal mandate and the professional responsibility of all teachers. The right of all students to participate in the regular classroom curriculum is protected by federal legislation (the Individuals with Disabilities Education Act, IDEA), and the progress of all students, including those who are English learners, students with disabilities, and students from poverty, must now be documented through requirements of the No Child Left Behind Act.

To be clear, however, we do not want to leave the impression that only children from poverty, or those with documented literacy difficulties, or those with learning disabilities labels, or those who are recent immigrants might be expected to find reading and learning from content text difficult. The reason for this book is that *all* children, regardless of background, need extra support comprehending content area material. Understanding content text requires readers to possess domain-specific knowledge of concepts and vocabulary. And it demands specialized approaches to processing and organizing ideas and information. For young children, these content-specific reading skills need to be scaffolded and take time to develop.

In order to provide responsive content literacy practices for all children, teachers need an extensive and flexible toolkit of strategies. Possessing such a toolkit is especially critical for teaching content area knowledge and skills (Braunger, Donahue, Evans, & Galguera, 2005; Fisher & Frey, 2001; Puckett & Brozo, 2005). Primary-grades teachers know that in order to be effective, they must scaffold literacy processes and strategies within actual reading and writing contexts, so children can use their literacy abilities with stories and informational passages in all subject areas throughout the school day (Wray, Medwell, Fox, & Poulson, 2000). Exemplary elementary teachers employ a range of literacy and learning strategies that can be integrated across the content areas (Allington & Johnston, 2002) and adapted to the differentiated needs of struggling learners (Taylor, Pearson, Clark, & Walpole, 2000).

Unfortunately, too many children of color (Ladson-Billings & Gomez, 2001; Jimenez, 1997) and those receiving special education services (Fisher, Schumaker, & Deshler, 2002) may not be getting adequate training in higher-level literacy skills. Nevertheless, students from diverse backgrounds can be taught to improve their reading and thinking abilities when knowledge of content area reading, language development, and learning strategies is applied to them as it is to their more successful peers (Dole, Brown, & Trathen, 1996; Wood & Algozzine, 1994) and, when appropriate, strategies are adapted to meet their unique learning needs (Pearman, Huang, & Mellblom, 1997).

Research has shown that technology is a powerful tool for helping readers better understand content texts (Leu, Kinzer, Coiro, & Cammack, 2004). It also provides students with the means for accessing literacy supports independently, within the curriculum task, and at the moment needed. Technology provides teachers with the ability to manage these supports for students with a wide variety of abilities, allowing more concentration on the content of the learning standard at hand. We demonstrate throughout this book how to use technology, not as a stand-alone activity, but as a tool for providing content area reading strategy supports.

The issue of helping teachers employ technology to develop students' literacy abilities has been addressed through recent legislation and is a continuing concern for policy makers. Furthermore, as we have indicated, the right for all students to participate in the regular classroom curriculum is protected by federal legislation (the Individuals with Disabilities Education Act [IDEA, 2004] and progress of all students is required by the No Child Left Behind Act. Technology is becoming a necessary tool for implementing the requirements of these legislative initiatives.

New technologies make unique instructional practices possible. Technology applications provide both teachers and learners with curriculum flexibility that was previously unattainable. Digital formats made possible by technology provide the means to change text to suit the learners' needs: It can be transformed, transported, or recorded. Similarly, technology allows students choices in expression of ideas: Voice, sound, pictures, and animation can accompany written words. Projects can be demonstrated in real time or viewed by others asynchronously, changing participation requirements. Material that is presented in a digital format can be linked to other information, thus providing supports and scaffolding for students with diverse learning abilities.

Designing lessons with strategic use of technology increases the probability that all students will be able to participate in the learning experience and reduces the need for elaborate adaptations and modifications of material later on (Rose & Meyer, 2000).

Research indicates that when students, regardless of ability, have access to multiple means of representation, expression, and engagement, participation in the curriculum increases (O'Neil, 2000). This method of technology use, referred to as *Universal Design for Learning (UDL),* can be paired with literacy strategies as an effective means of expanding content area knowledge for all students. In Chapter 3 we will further develop aspects of universal design, demonstrating the utility of this approach for content literacy and learning.

THINK and APPLY

For content literacy-technology connections to occur, you must be knowledge-able of strategies and develop familiarity with software tools. To determine the status of your current knowledge and use, please respond to the items below by checking whether you're "familiar" with the strategy or technology application, "use" the strategy or technology, or "not familiar" with the strategy or technology application.

Content Literacy Strategies	Familiar	Use	Not Familiar
1. KWL	____	____	____
2. Anticipation guide	____	____	____
3. SQPL	____	____	____
4. Lesson impression	____	____	____
5. GISTing	____	____	____
6. QAR	____	____	____
7. Process guide	____	____	____
8. Word grid	____	____	____
9. RAFT writing	____	____	____
10. SPAWN writing	____	____	____
11. Reader-response writing	____	____	____

List three ways you can gain more knowledge and skills of these content literacy strategies.

1. _____

2. _____

3. _____

Content Literacy Strategies	Familiar	Use	Not Familiar
1. Inspiration	____	___	____
2. Kidspiration	____	___	____
3. Kurzweil	____	___	____
4. Intellitalk	____	___	____
5. Visual learning programs	____	___	____
6. Presentation programs	____	___	____
7. Hand helds	____	___	____

List three ways you can gain more knowledge and skills of these computer technology tools.

1. _____

2. _____

3. _____

Considerations for Learners with Special Needs: Assistive and Instructional Technology

Although one of our overarching themes is that technology applications can increase content literacy and learning for all students, we also know that technology may be necessary for students with disabilities who would otherwise experience barriers to academic progress. When technology is used for this puropose, it is referred to as *assistive technology (AT)*. This special application of technology is defined by IDEA (2004) as "any item, piece of equipment, or product system, whether acquired commercially off the shelf, modified, or customized, that is used to increase, maintain, or improve functional capabilities of individuals with disabilities" (20 U.S. C. 1401 [24]).

Assistive technology can refer to a broad range of devices that may or may not be designed specifically with individuals with disabilities in mind. The key to referring to a form of technology as assistive is the extent to which it allows a student with disabilities to accomplish tasks that would otherwise be difficult or impossible. For example, consider the hand-held electronic dictionary, a form of technology in general use. For most students, this device is merely a convenient and efficient tool for determining the definition of unknown words and is considered to be an instructional use of technology. The electronic dictionary, however, is considered to be an assistive technology device in the hands of a student with disabilities who is struggling with reading. This device displays a definition that can be read aloud using text-to-speech features, allowing the student to participate meaningfully in word study activities. Many such applications blur the distinction between technology use that is considered assistive and that which is considered instructional and could benefit any student, regardless of ability. In other words, most technology tools, when used appropriately by teachers and students, have the potential to benefit every learner, as is the case with the technology applications found in Chapters 4 through 7.

Assistive technology should be considered for every student with disabilities during the individual educational plan (IEP) process. Among the difficulties in implementing this requirement is the extent (or lack thereof) of the knowledge base that individuals possess about technology. Classroom teachers and

15

Content Literacy
and Technology:
A Twenty-first–
Century Approach
for Children with
Diverse Abilities

special educators cannot consider the possible applications of technology that they do not understand. This paradox of consideration (Edyburn, 2003) typically results in technology being recommended for only the most obvious needs, while the array of technology software applications for other students with diverse abilities, for whom technology can greatly assist in content literacy development, remain generally unconsidered.

Ironically, much of the technology that could be considered by IEP teams is readily met by instructional technologies available in most classrooms. These applications are relatively easy to use and adaptable to general education curriculum content. Factors hindering consideration appear to be related to a lack of knowledge by general and special education teachers alike (Puckett, 2004) about how to use technology to support literacy. Furthermore, the requirement for AT consideration, made by the IEP team on an individual student basis, typically results in equipment or software assigned for the exclusive use of that student. A more efficient strategy would be for teachers to have access to a "toolkit" of software and equipment that could be quickly deployed as needed for any and all students in the support of literacy and content learning tasks (Edyburn, 2000).

Although suggestions for the use of instructional and assistive technology in support of content literacy learning are appearing with increasing regularity in the literature (Edyburn, 2003; Hitchcock, Meyer, Rose, & Jackson, 2002, Castellani & Jeffs, 2001), few actual classroom examples are extant. In succeeding chapters you will see numerous envisionments of classroom teachers employing a toolkit to craft instruction that pairs technology with content area literacy strategies to meet the reading, writing, and learning needs of all students.

Looking Back

By now you have a clearer idea of the need for new and innovative approaches for helping children grow in their ability to use reading and writing in the service of content learning. One such way to accomplish this is by taking advantage of computer technology for teaching content literacy strategies and skills. As you discovered, this combination results in highly engaging and interactive learning experiences for today's children who are comfortable with and motivated by digital technology. Federal law requires that all children be given the opportunity and tools to meet common curricular standards in language arts, social studies, science, and math. Meeting these standards is made easier for children of diverse abilities when computer technology serves as the medium of exposure, prompts interactive reading, writing, and thinking, and is adaptable to individual needs.

Questions For Study

- In the "Think and Apply" box of this chapter you were asked to determine the status of your knowledge and skills related to content literacy strategies and computer technology and then think of three ways to increase your knowledge and skills in these areas. Continue that conversation with your colleagues. What is the status of their skills set and toolkits? What ideas do they have for gaining a better understanding of and practical experience with content literacy and computer technology?

- Individually or as a group or committee explore your school and/or district for available resources that could be used to increase knowledge of and skills with content literacy and computer technology. Who could serve as technology expert or advisor? Who could provide professional development in content literacy? What software products and licenses does the school or district own? What assistive technology hardware/software is available and in use?

17

Content Literacy
and Technology:
A Twenty-First–
Century Approach
for Children with
Diverse Abilities

References

Allington, R. L., & Johnston, P. (2002). *Reading to learn: Lessons from exemplary 4th grade classrooms.* New York: Guilford.

Alvermann, D., Swafford, J., & Montero, M. K. (2004). *Reading for information in elementary school: Content literacy strategies to build comprehension.* Boston: Addison-Wesley.

Battistich, V., Solomon, D., Kim, D., Watson, M., & Schaps, E. (1995). Schools as communities, poverty levels of student populations, and student attitudes, motives, and performance: A multilevel analysis. *American Educational Research Journal, 32,* 627–658.

Behrmann, M., & Jerome, M. K. (2002). *Assistive technology for students with mild disabilities: Update 2002.* ERIC Digest E623. ERIC Document Reproduction Service ED 463 595.

Berliner, D. (2006). Our impoverished view of educational reform. *Teachers College Record, 108,* 949–995.

Braunger, J., Donahue, D., Evans, K., & Galguera, T. (2005). *Rethinking preparation for content area teaching: The reading apprenticeship approach.* San Francisco: Jossey-Bass.

Brozo, W. G., & Simpson, M. L. (2007). *Content literacy for today's adolescents: Honoring diversity and building competence.* Upper Saddle River, NJ: Merrill/Prentice-Hall.

Castellani, J., & Jeffs, T. (2001). Emerging reading and writing strategies using technology. *Teaching Exceptional Children, 33*(5), 60–67.

Caswell, L., & Duke, N. (1998). Non-narrative as a catalyst for literacy development. *Language Arts, 75,* 108–117.

Dole, J., Brown, K., & Trathen, W. (1996). The effects of strategy instruction on the comprehension performance of at-risk students. *Reading Research Quarterly, 31,* 62–88.

Duke, N. K. (2000). 3.6 minutes per day: The scarcity of informational texts in first grade. *Reading Research Quarterly, 35*(2), 202–224.

Duke, N. K., & Bennett-Armistead, V. S. (2003). *Reading and writing*

informational text in the primary grades: Research-based practices.
New York: Scholastic.

Duncan, G. J., & Brooks-Dunn, J. (1997). *Consequences of growing up poor.* New York: Russell Sage.

Duncan, G. L., & Seymour, P. H. (2000). Socioeconomic differences in foundation level literacy. *British Journal of Psychology, 91,* 145–166.

Edyburn, D. (2003). Reading difficulties in the general education classroom: A taxonomy of text modification strategies. *Closing the Gap, 21*(6), 1, 10–13, 30–31.

Edyburn, D. L. (2000). Assistive technology and students with mild disabilities. *Focus on Exceptional Children, 32*(9), 1–23.

Fisher, D., & Frey, N. (2006). *Content area literacy instruction for the elementary grades.* Upper Saddle River, NJ: Merrill/Prentice-Hall.

Fisher, D., & Frey, N. (2001). Access to the core curriculum: Critical ingredients for success. *Remedial and Special Education, 22,* 148–157.

Fisher, J., Schumaker, J., & Deshler, D. (2002). Improving the reading comprehension of at-risk adolescents. In C. C. Block & M. Pressley (Eds.), *Comprehension instruction: Research-based best practices* (pp. 351–364). New York: Guilford.

Francis, D. J., Shaywitz, S. E., Stuebing, K. K., Shaywitz, B. A., & Fletcher, J. M. (1996). Developmental lag versus deficit models of reading disability: A longitudinal, individual growth curves analysis. *Journal of Educational Psychology, 88,* 3–17.

Hawkins, M. R. (2004). Researching English language and literacy development in schools. *Educational Researcher, 33,* 14–25.

Hitchock, C., Meyer, A., Rose, D., & Jackson, R. (2002). Providing new access to the general curriculum: Universal design for learning. *Teaching Exceptional Children, 35*(2), 8–17.

Individuals with Disabilities Education Improvement Act. (2004). Public Law 108-446 (20 U.S.C.1400 *et seq.*). Retrieved November 4, 2006, from http://edworkforce.house.gov/issues/108th/education/idea/conferencereport/confrept/htm.

International Reading Association. (2001). Integrating literacy and technology in the curriculum. Retrieved September 30, 2007 from www.reading.org/downloads/positions/ps1048_technology.pdf.

19

Content Literacy
and Technology:
A Twenty-First–
Century Approach
for Children with
Diverse Abilities

Jimenez, R. (1997). The strategic reading abilities and potential of five low-literacy Latina/o readers in middle school. *Reading Research Quarterly, 32,* 224–243.

Kaplan, M. W. & Edyburn, D. L. (1998). Essential tools of the trade: An assistive technology specialist shares her tool kit. *Closing the Gap, 17*(3), 1, 8, 18, 24.

Kinzer, C. K. (2003, June). The importance of recognizing the expanding boundaries of literacy. *Reading Online, 6*(10). Available: www.readingonline.org/electronic/elec_index.asp?HREF=/electronic/kinzer/index.html.

Kleiner, A., & Farris, E. (2002, September). *Internet access in U.S. public schools and classrooms: 1994–2001.* Washington, DC: Department of Education, National Center for Education Statistics.

Ladson-Billings, G., & Gomez, M. L. (2001). Just showing up: Supporting early literacy through teachers' professional communities. *Phi Delta Kappan, 82,* 75–80.

Leu, D. J. (2000). Literacy and technology: Deictic consequences for literacy education in an information age. In M. Kamil, P. Mosenthal, P. D. Pearson, & R. Barr (Eds.), *Handbooks of reading research* (vol. III, pp. 743–770). Mahwah, NJ: Erlbaum.

Leu, D. J., Kinzer, C. K., Coiro, J. L., & Cammack, D. W. (2004). Toward a theory of new literacies emerging from the Internet and other information and communication technologies. In R. Ruddell & N. Unrau (Eds.), *Theoretical models and processes of reading* (5th ed.). Newark, DE: International Reading Association.

Loschert, K. (2003). High-tech teaching. *Tomorrow's Teachers, 9,* 2–5.

National Assessment for Educational Progress. (2002). *The nation's report card* [online]. Retrieved September 25, 2003 from http://nces.ed.gov/nationsreportcard/.

National Center for Educational Evaluation. (2007). *Effectiveness of reading and mathematics software products: Findings from the first student cohort.* Washington, DC: U.S. Department of Education. Retrieved August 15, 2007 from http://ies.ed.gov/ncee/pdf/20074006.pdf.

Newman, J. M. (2000). Following the yellow brick road. *Phi Delta Kappan, 81,* 774–779.

Norris, C. A., & Soloway, E. M. (2003). The viable alternative: Handhelds. *School Administrator*, *60*(4), 26–28.

O'Brien, D. G. (2001). "At-risk" adolescents: Redefining competence through the multiliteracies of intermediality, visual arts, and representation. *Reading Online*, *4*(11). Available: www.readingonline .org/newliteracies/lit_Index.asp?HREF=/newliteracies/obrien/ index.html.

O'Neil, L. (2000). Computer technology can empower students with learning disabilities. *Exceptional Parent*, *30*(7), 72–74.

Pearman, E., Huang, A., & Mellblom, C. (1997). The inclusion of all students: Concerns and incentives of educators. *Education and Training in Mental Retardation and Development*, *32*, 11–19.

Pearson, G., & Young, A. T. (2002). Technically speaking: Why all Americans need to know more about technology. *The Technology Teacher*, *62*, 8–12.

Puckett, K. (2004). Project ACCESS: Field testing an assistive technology toolkit for students with mild disabilities. *Journal of Special Education Technology*, *19*, 5–18.

Puckett, K., & Brozo, W. G. (2005). Using assistive technology to teach content area literacy strategies to students with disabilities. In J. R. Dugan, P. Linder, M. B. Sampson, B. Brancato, & L. Elish-Piper (Eds.), *Celebrating the power of literacy: College Reading Association Yearbook* (pp. 462–479). Commerce, TX: Texas A&M University–Commerce.

Richardson, J. (2004, July/August). Content area literacy lessons go high tech. *Reading Online*, *8*(1). Available: www.readingonline .org/articles/art_index.asp?HREF=richardson/index.html.

Rose, D., & Meyer, A. (2000). Universal design for individual differences. *Educational Leadership*, *58*(3), 39–43.

Rozell, E. J., & Garnder, W. L. (2000). Cognitive, motivation, and affective processes associated with computer related performance: A path analysis. *Computers in Human Behavior*, *16*, 199–222.

Shaywitz, S. (2003). *Overcoming dyslexia: A new and complete science-based program for reading problems at any level*. New York: Knopf.

Sølvberg, A. (2003). Computer-related control beliefs and motivation: A panel study. *Journal of Research on Technology in Education*, *35*, 473–487.

Content Literacy
and Technology:
A Twenty-First–
Century Approach
for Children with
Diverse Abilities

Songer, N. B., Lee, H., & Kam, R. (2002). Technology-rich inquiry science in urban classrooms: What are the barriers to inquiry pedagogy? *Journal of Research in Science Teaching, 39*, 128–150.

Stanovich, K. E. (1986). Matthew effects in reading: Some consequences of individual differences in the development of reading fluency. *Reading Research Quarterly, 16*, 32–71.

Taylor, B. M., Pearson, P. D., Clark, K., & Walpole, S. (2000). Effective schools and accomplished teachers: Lessons about primary grade reading instruction in low income schools. *Elementary School Journal, 101*, 121–165.

Tileston, D. W. (2004). *What every teacher should know about media and technology*. Thousand Oaks, CA: Corwin.

U.S. Census Bureau. (2001). *Home computers and Internet use in the United States: August 2000*. Retrieved September 5, 2005, from www.census.gov/prod/2001pubs/p23-207.pdf.

Wood, K., & Algozzine, B. (1994). *Teaching reading to high-risk learners: A unified perspective*. Boston: Allyn and Bacon.

Wray, D., Medwell, J., Fox, R., & Poulson, L. (2000). The teaching practices of effective teachers of literacy. *Educational Review, 62*, 75–84.

Content Literacy and Learning Strategies

Seeing Forward

After reading Chapter 1 you now have a better understanding about how technology can positively impact students' academic lives and better prepare them to be engaged citizens of the twenty-first century. As schools become increasingly diverse, it is the responsibility of every teacher to use the best practices available to meet the range of reading and learning needs these young people bring to the classroom. In this chapter, we describe and exemplify several evidence-based content literacy strategies organized within a simple instructional framework. These strategies have been proven to engage diverse youth in interactive experiences that build essential skills, promote and sustain encounters with print and text, and expand access to content area information and ideas. These content literacy strategies also allow students to create new knowledge and express new understandings. Each one will reappear in subsequent chapters as integrated lessons with technology applications.

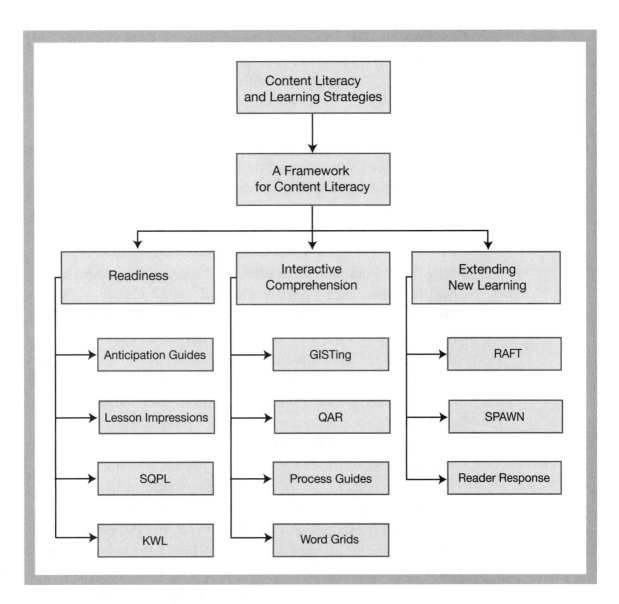

Overview of Content Literacy and Learning Strategies

Let's begin by considering the skills and competencies inherent in academic literacy. *Academic literacy* has come to refer to the reading, writing, speaking, listening, and viewing skills needed to accomplish school-based tasks (Brozo & Simpson, 2007; Fisher & Ivey, 2005). As compared with everyday literacy practices youth engage in, such as reading the Sunday comics, instant messaging friends, or following assembly directions for a new toy, academic literacy requires knowledge of specialized vocabulary, sustained attention to details and big ideas, the ability to organize and analyze print and visual data, and the ability to compose structured essays and reports.

The literacy demands placed on youth by the volume and variety of content texts and tasks, which increase dramatically in the intermediate grades, are the principal reasons for the phenomenon called the *fourth-grade slump* (Cummins, 2001; McCray, Vaughn, & Neal, 2001; Snow, 2002). Many children who have progressed normally in reading up to that time will find themselves struggling to understand and generate increasingly complex narratives and expository texts. Along with a decline in achievement comes a dip in motivation to read and learn (Eccles et al., 1993). For children who have not progressed normally in reading and writing through the primary grades or who are English learners, the challenges of acquiring academic literacy abilities necessary for success in science, math, social studies, and all other subjects can seem especially daunting.

Literacy strategies and practices to support students' acquisition of content information and concepts have been around for a long time, with many new variations and twists. The research basis for content literacy is strong but tells more about principles and guidelines to follow than specific techniques and practices (Sturtevant et al., 2006). Consequently, only content literacy strategies that adhere to evidence-based principles have been included in this chapter. These strategies will be further developed with technology applications in subsequent chapters.

A Framework for Content Literacy

It has become logical and productive to organize content literacy strategies around the three main phases of a lesson.

Phase I: Readiness

Every good lesson in any discipline begins with practices to activate and build students' relevant prior knowledge, capture their interest and motivate them to read and learn, and help them set meaningful purposes for learning about the topic (Brozo, 2003, 2004; Guthrie & Humenick, 2004). The best readiness strategies also have a recursive feature. What is meant by this is that they not only initiate the lesson but are structured in ways that require students to return repeatedly throughout the lesson to what was begun in readiness. In the next section we'll describe four highly effective readiness strategies that have this recursive element: anticipation guides, lesson impressions, student questions for purposeful learning (SQPL), and KWL.

Phase II: Interactive Comprehension

As students encounter information and ideas from various text sources on the topic under consideration in a content lesson, they need strategies that support their efforts at constructive meaning making (Bean, 2000; Caccamise, 2005; Pressley, 2000). Later in this chapter we'll share four such strategies: GISTing, question-answer relations (QAR), process guides, and word grids.

Phase III: Extending New Learning

To make new learning permanent and provide students with opportunities to elaborate and generate new understandings (Wittrock, 1990), students should be exposed to strategies that require writing and responding in meaningful and creative ways (Santa & Havens, 1991; Sorcinelli & Elbow, 1997). The best ones in our experience and the experience of disciplinary teachers with whom we've worked around the country are RAFT, SPAWN, and reader-response writing, which will be discussed in this chapter.

Readiness	Interactive Comprehension	Extending New Learning
■ Anticipation Guides	■ GISTing	■ RAFT Writing
■ Lesson Impressions	■ QAR	■ SPAWN Writing
■ SQPL	■ Process Guides	■ Reader Response Writing
■ KWL	■ Word Grids	

Readiness Strategies for Content Literacy and Learning

Anticipation Guides

A highly regarded strategy for activating prior knowledge of new topics and helping students set purposes for reading and learning is the *anticipation guide.* This strategy involves giving students a list of statements about the topic to be studied and asking them to respond to the statements before a full exploration of the information sources. Guides are particularly useful when they provoke disagreement and challenge students' beliefs. They should force students to think closely about their prior knowledge for a topic and lead to clarification of any misconceptions (Duffelmeyer & Baum, 1992; Merkley, 1996/97; White & Johnson, 2001). This function seems especially important, given research evidence indicating that students' existing prior knowledge and biases will be superimposed on text information when the two are at odds (Marshall, 1989). In other words, if misconceptions about a topic are not cleared up during reading and learning, they may still exist afterward.

Anticipation guides should contain statements drawn from important information and ideas from the various sources used to explore the topic. In addition, Duffelmeyer (1994) recommends the inclusion of certain statements that force students to reconsider existing beliefs. He suggests that four kinds of statements have the potential to do this: (1) those that are related to the major ideas students will encounter, (2) those that activate students' prior knowledge, (3) those that are general rather than specific, and (4) those that challenge students' beliefs. We recommend that guide statements be written to appear correct but incompatible with the information students will encounter or to seem incorrect yet compatible with the information to follow.

The response format for anticipation guides can vary. As you will see in Chapter 6, guides are highly amenable to computer-generated displays with interactive functions. Regardless of how anticipation guides are structured and presented, students should not be asked to write extended responses to guide statements, like they're typically asked to do with the all-too-familiar and often unmotivating discussion or essay questions. Instead, have students respond with simple check marks or brief responses to guide statements. What make anticipation guides enticing are their novel formats. And just because the student responses are short, their thinking about the topic isn't limited. Nonetheless, an accountability feature that requires students to verify their responses after reading and encountering new content can be incorporated into an anticipation guide. This guards against students making random responses without careful thinking (Duffelmeyer & Baum, 1992).

Look at the anticipation guide designed for a consumer business class shown in Figure 2.1. We constructed this example using the tables feature of a standard word processor. If students had been assigned this anticipation guide for an upcoming

FIGURE 2.1

Anticipation Guide for Buying and Selling a Car

Directions: Read each statement below then decide whether you agree (A) or disagree (D) with it by placing a check in the appropriate "Before" column. After reading and learning about the topic, reread each statement and put a check in the appropriate "After" column. Be sure to write a sentence summarizing what you learned about each statement in support of your "After" reading and learning response.

1. When buying a car it is good to know the dealer cost.	Before		After	
	A	D	A	D
What did you learn?				

2. The sticker price on the car is the final price.	Before		After	
	A	D	A	D
What did you learn?				

3. Used cars have a cheaper monthly payment than new cars.	Before		After	
	A	D	A	D
What did you learn?				

4. It is smarter to buy a used car than a new car.	Before		After	
	A	D	A	D
What did you learn?				

5. Dealer cost is more than retail cost.	Before		After	
	A	D	A	D
What did you learn?				

6. The suggested retail price is what the dealer has to sell the car for in order to make a profit.	Before		After	
	A	D	A	D
What did you learn?				

7. Ten percent markup is a reasonable profit for selling a car.	Before		After	
	A	D	A	D
What did you learn?				

reading assignment or lecture on buying and selling a car, they should be allowed first to meet in small groups and then, with the entire class, to discuss their viewpoints and share information and ideas. As students debate and defend their "Before" reading and learning responses, the teacher should remain neutral by not giving away answers or taking over the discussion. Periodically, the teacher should restate points of view or try to clarify ideas.

The accountability feature of this guide asks students to indicate what they learned from the information sources that helped them finally decide whether to agree or disagree with each statement. During reading and exploration of a topic, as students encounter information related to the statements, they should indicate whether the text or lecture material supports or does not support their "Before" column indications. Support for their choices "After" reading and learning would come in the form of a brief written statement summarizing what they learned. Students might also be asked to provide a page number from a textbook, or class note entries. It adds further learning potential to the activity by forcing self-interrogation and more elaborative interaction with the text.

As you can see, the anticipation guide takes advantage of prediction as a powerful readiness to learn tool. Guesses, in this case, serve as predictions. Then, as students read and study information about buying and selling cars, they will return to the guide statements and verify the correctness or incorrectness of their initial responses. The guide statements should focus on the key issues and points of the topic. They should force students to think about what they already know and believe about a topic and then confirm, modify, or disconfirm existing beliefs. Working with anticipation guides helps create the urge in students to know more. They confront the topic ideas and information purposefully and enthusiastically (Hurst, 2001; Strange & Wyant, 1999). And by forcing students to make and defend predictions, guides can help sustain interest in topics; promote active listening, reading, and discussion; and facilitate assimilation of new information into existing schema.

Another advantage of anticipation guides is that they can be prepared very quickly and without extensive planning or time-consuming clerical tasks. The guide statements require the most effort to compose, but can be crafted during planning periods or even before class. Once the statements are developed, they can be presented to students in a variety of ways. For example, "True/ False" or "Agree/Disagree" can be placed in the "Before" column to the *left* of each statement. To the *right* of the statements, place the same response options in the "After" column. Below each statement, students can write supporting information, such as a summary of the relevant information or the page and paragraph number where the information was found.

Using a computer-mediated anticipation guide increases your instructional flexibility. The guide can be printed for each student, displayed using a projections system, or saved as a template and loaded on computer workstations for students to complete and submit for feedback in either print or electronic formats.

Lesson Impressions

For this strategy, students are given just enough information about the topic to activate prior knowledge and develop an "impression." They are then asked to write or discuss their impressions of the forthcoming lesson, which serve as predictions to be compared with the actual content. Lesson impressions can be used before exposing students to content regardless of the information sources. In other words, this readiness strategy is equally effective for a short story in English, a lecture in math, a guest speaker in history, a video in health, a CD in music, a field trip in art, or an experiment in science. Lesson impressions, like its relative story impressions (Denner, 2003; McGinley & Denner, 1987), can increase motivation by heightening anticipation and providing a meaningful purpose for learning (Brozo, 2004; Guthrie & Humenick, 2004).

Conducting a lesson impression involves first extracting words and phrases from the material to be covered and presenting these in the order in which they will be encountered to students. The words should be related to the information and ideas you consider most important for students to consider in advance of full exploration of the topic.

The next step is to have students write or discuss with a partner what they think they are about to learn by composing a short description or narrative in which all of the words are used. When students finish writing or orally sharing, they should be asked to read or tell the class their impressions. In this way, they can compare and contrast one another's predictions about the content to be covered in the upcoming lesson. The goal is to gather a variety of impressions so that students are left with a sense that theirs or any one of their classmates may be the most accurate. This process will heighten their anticipation.

Teachers can use a number of technology resources in constructing lesson impression activities. Typing the key words into a word-processing or presentation program will maximize time and efficiency in developing presentation and student materials. A simple strategy is to develop a worksheet with the words listed above or below the writing space. This "worksheet" could be used with partial sentences, and saved as a template for student use at computer stations or laptops. Once entered into a word processor, the words could be "sent" (without retyping) to a PowerPoint presentation or other multimedia program. Students can then compose their sentences on each slide by typing, adding a voice note, or using the speech recognition option. They also have access to graphics capacities to illustrate their intent.

At this point, students are ready for the information sources. As they receive and explore the content they should pay particular attention to how what they're learning compares with their readiness phase impressions. This can be best accomplished by pausing periodically during the lesson and asking students to reflect on what they've learned relative to what they thought they would learn. Some teachers require students to keep a record of the similarities and differences between their impressions and the actual content by creating a Venn diagram or a compare/contrast chart. We recommend such practices because they add an accountability feature that raises the level of assurance that students are remaining engaged throughout the lesson. Figure 2.2 presents lesson impression words for a read-aloud

Figure 2.2

Lesson Impression Words, Student Story, and Venn Diagram

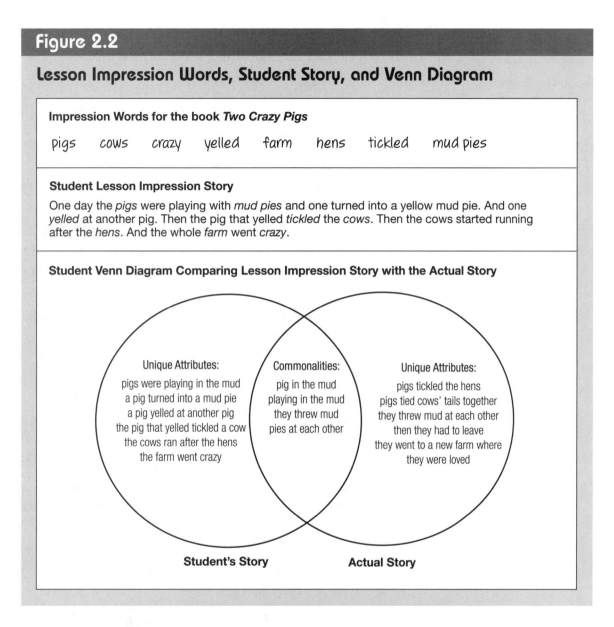

Impression Words for the book *Two Crazy Pigs*

pigs   cows   crazy   yelled   farm   hens   tickled   mud pies

Student Lesson Impression Story

One day the *pigs* were playing with *mud pies* and one turned into a yellow mud pie. And one *yelled* at another pig. Then the pig that yelled *tickled* the *cows*. Then the cows started running after the *hens*. And the whole *farm* went *crazy*.

Student Venn Diagram Comparing Lesson Impression Story with the Actual Story

Unique Attributes:
pigs were playing in the mud
a pig turned into a mud pie
a pig yelled at another pig
the pig that yelled tickled a cow
the cows ran after the hens
the farm went crazy

Commonalities:
pig in the mud
playing in the mud
they threw mud
pies at each other

Unique Attributes:
pigs tickled the hens
pigs tied cows' tails together
they threw mud at each other
then they had to leave
they went to a new farm where
they were loved

Student's Story   **Actual Story**

story in language arts class. Before sharing the read-aloud book, *Two Crazy Pigs* (Nagel, 1992), students wrote stories based on the words, then created a Venn diagram using the software program Inspiration to compare and contrast their impression stories with the actual events of the book. Figure 2.2 includes a sample student story and a student Venn diagram.

A science teacher presented his students with the following words, which they accessed from a file on their laptop computers:

space ship   planet   atmosphere   protective gear   hostile

terrain   gravity   specimens   exploration

Next, he asked his students to use their laptops to write for five to seven minutes using as many of these words as possible in their short compositions. The teacher told the students that they should write what they expected to hear during the upcoming presentation on exploration of the planets in the solar system. He urged students to be creative, incorporating the words in a song, poem, or story.

Many of the students wrote what they knew about planetary exploration, which helped the teacher discover the extent of their prior knowledge. Others, who were more comfortable with the content, chose to be creative and were eager to share their work before the presentation began. The teacher found his students paying closer attention during the lesson. Since they had not yet submitted their compositions, several students corrected their stories with the information they gleaned from the presentation. The lesson impression strategy had engendered focused listening and heightened motivation to learn due to students' desire to compare their impression texts with the content of the teacher's presentation.

One student's lesson impression composition read:

As I descended from the *space ship*, I began to feel the chill of the *planet*'s *atmosphere*. It was too cold to live without *protective gear*. I thought that it would be cold so far from the sun, but not this cold. I took out my gun—this was a *hostile* place. I began to explore the hard *terrain*. Luckily, there was little *gravity*, so I moved easily. I discovered the rocks were a color I

> never seen before on Earth, kind of a cross between
> purple and orange. I took some *specimens* and contin-
> ued my *exploration*.

When the science teacher asked his students at the end of the
class period what they liked or disliked about the strategy, their
responses were consistent. They liked the freedom to be creative
and they thought the lesson impression activity helped them
focus more closely on information about the planets.

Student Questions for Purposeful Learning (SQPL)

The SQPL readiness strategy was developed out of the need to
help students become more active, generative learners (Brozo &
Simpson, 2007; Fisher, Brozo, Frey, & Ivey, 2007). Often, teachers supply information and questions during readiness, whereas
SQPL induces students to generate their own questions and then
to explore the content closely for answers. The strategy prompts
students to ask questions before reading and learning that are
important to them. In this way, they heighten anticipation and
engage in more purposeful reading and learning (Ediger &
Pavlik, 1999; Guthrie & Wigfield, 2000; Schunk & Zimmerman,
1998) as they search for answers to their questions.

The first step entails crafting a thought-provoking statement
and presenting it to students. Here is a statement given to a math
class about to study a unit on trigonometry:

> With just a yardstick and a shadow, you can measure the
> distance around the entire Earth.

The next step is to allow students to pair up and brainstorm
questions they would like to have answered based on the statement. In the math class students were asked to turn to their
neighbor and come up with three questions about the statement.
Afterward, the teacher elicited the students' questions and listed

them on the board. The goal in this step is to gather a variety of questions, making sure each student pair contributes at least one of its questions. We recommend that you highlight or star questions asked by more than one pair of students; these become class consensus questions. You can also consolidate questions by combining similar ones.

After every student had an opportunity to add a question to the total, the math teacher drew the class's attention to those questions that were essentially the same, and added stars next to those questions. Some questions, such as *How do you measure the size of the Earth?* had five stars, since at least five separate pairs of students came up with the same or highly similar question. Another question, *Why is the shadow so important?* was repeated four times, and *How do mathematicians measure the Earth today?* had three stars.

At this stage, students are ready for the presentation of the information. Like anticipation guides and lesson impressions, SQPL is adaptable to virtually any information source, such as textbook or story reading, lecture, discussion, video, field trip, and the Internet. Students in the math class were directed to pay very close attention to information that answers the questions the class generated, especially class consensus questions. It is important to point out that student-generated readiness questions should not be the only perspectives students have of the content. This strategy should be one strategy among many and should not comprise the overall exploration of the topic. It helps students make an investment in the learning process, since they become gatherers of information based on their own inquiry and not on prompts given them by the teacher or the textbook (Rosenshine, Meister, & Chapman, 1996). Nonetheless, student questions may fail to cover critical information. Therefore, you may need to contribute your own questions based on the SQPL prompt to ensure that all important aspects of the topic are considered by students.

KWL

Like SQPL, KWL activates students' relevant prior knowledge and elicits questions from them before reading and learning (Carr & Ogle, 1987; Ogle, 1992). Then, as students progress through the lesson, they identify answers to the questions they generated about the topic in readiness. The letters of the strategy stand for (1) what I already *know (K)* about the topic; (2) what I *want (W)* to know about the topic, expressed in the form of questions; and (3) what I *learned (L)* about the topic as a result of the lesson, in particular, what I found in answer to my questions.

The appropriate recursive elements in KWL make it especially useful as a readiness strategy. Before reading, the student activates background knowledge and sets a purpose for reading by generating questions (Beck, McKeown, Hamilton, & Kucan, 1997; Huffman, 2000); during reading, the student thinks critically about information and monitors learning relative to the guiding questions; and after reading, the student integrates and consolidates the information read. Here, we focus on the before-reading benefits of the strategy.

To give you a better idea of the kind of thinking involved in the KWL strategy, let us assume you were asked in a professional development workshop or university class to employ the KWL strategy for Chapter 2, the chapter you are reading now. First, you would be directed to read the title, "Content Literacy and Learning Strategies," and in small cooperative groups or as a whole class, you would brainstorm and discuss ideas and information you already hold in prior knowledge about the topic. Through discussion, a good deal of known information will be generated, and unresolved points and unanswered questions also will likely emerge. These will be saved and referred to later as issues about which you desire further information. So, after brainstorming and discussing, you would have a collection of ideas and facts about the chapter topic listed on a chart or on computer screens in the *K* (what is *known*) column.

In the next phase before reading, you would be asked to generate questions you would like answered by Chapter 2. Questions come from the brainstorming and discussion, as well as anticipated information you think will be encountered in the text. These questions comprise the entries in the second column on the chart: *W* (what you *want* to learn). By developing questions in this way, you will tend to define for yourself your purpose for reading. The result is that your reading and self-monitoring during reading will be more focused. As you read, you will pause periodically to monitor your comprehension by checking the questions from the *W* column that can be answered by what you have read. As new information is encountered, additional questions can be added to the list. Thus, purposes are refined and extended throughout reading.

Figure 2.3 depicts what you might have generated for the first two columns of the KWL chart. As you read, you would note in the *L* column new information and information that helps answer the questions you posed in the *W* column. After reading, you would be asked to discuss what you have learned from your reading. You would review the questions asked before and during reading to determine if and how they were answered. For example, the first four questions in the *W* column can be answered fairly thoroughly with the information in this chapter. For the last question, which would remain unresolved because this chapter does not specifically discuss application of the strategies using computer technology, you would be encouraged to consult subsequent chapters or conduct some personal research to gather further information about this aspect of the topic. Perhaps the professor or workshop director would direct you to additional content literacy books or to journal articles that deal with the topic of technology and literacy strategies.

The KWL strategy can be applied in a variety of content areas with a range of text material (Marchand-Martella, Wasta, & Martella, 1996). Figure 2.4, for example, is a KWL chart created

Figure 2.3

KWL for Chapter 2

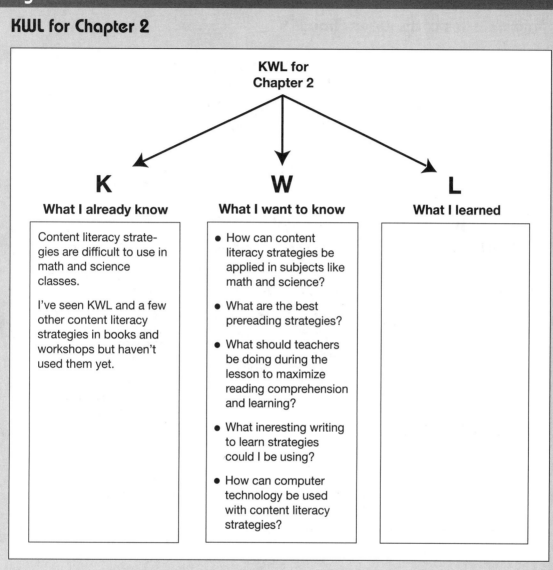

KWL for
Chapter 2

K

What I already know

Content literacy strategies are difficult to use in math and science classes.

I've seen KWL and a few other content literacy strategies in books and workshops but haven't used them yet.

W

What I want to know

- How can content literacy strategies be applied in subjects like math and science?

- What are the best prereading strategies?

- What should teachers be doing during the lesson to maximize reading comprehension and learning?

- What ineresting writing to learn strategies could I be using?

- How can computer technology be used with content literacy strategies?

L

What I learned

by a student in a physical education class about to study the major muscles of the upper body. In this example, note that the student appeared to have little prior knowledge for the topic. As a result of a liberal exchange of ideas in small groups and with

Figure 2.4

Major Muscles of the Upper Body

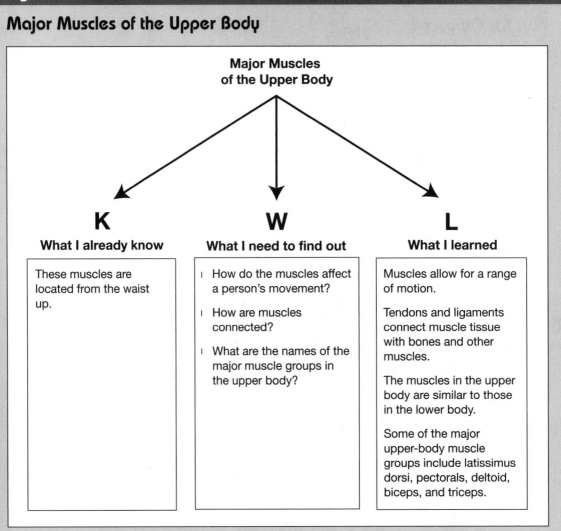

Major Muscles
of the Upper Body

K
What I already know

These muscles are located from the waist up.

W
What I need to find out

ı How do the muscles affect a person's movement?

ı How are muscles connected?

ı What are the names of the major muscle groups in the upper body?

L
What I learned

Muscles allow for a range of motion.

Tendons and ligaments connect muscle tissue with bones and other muscles.

The muscles in the upper body are similar to those in the lower body.

Some of the major upper-body muscle groups include latissimus dorsi, pectorals, deltoid, biceps, and triceps.

the whole class, the student asked some excellent questions (in the *W* column) that were answered by the reading. In cases in which students' questions cannot be answered by the text, many teachers will ask students to pursue answers to these questions through research and present their findings to the class.

Students will develop the ability to use the KWL strategy on their own through instruction that gradually shifts responsibility for initiating the strategy from you to your students (Schmidt, 1999). After you introduce the strategy with a textbook example and model KWL thinking by describing how you would develop a chart, you should ask students to implement it on their own. As with most content literacy and learning strategies, you can improve the likelihood that students will use the KWL strategy on their own if you demonstrate how it activates prior knowledge and sets purposes for reading and learning, facilitates their class performance, and helps them meet your expectations for learning.

In the preceding examples, SQPL and KWL charts can be produced using the software program Kidspiration or its companion program for older students, Inspiration. This visual learning program has a number of ready-made templates, such as a KWL chart, that can be easily adapted for any subject area. The program also gives the choice of exporting the content in an outline form into a word processor to assist in writing organization. A standard word processor could also be used to demonstrate these strategies. The content can be added spontaneously and interactively for all to see by using a computer projection system or interactive white board (such as a SMART board).

Interactive Comprehension Strategies

GISTing

The ability to summarize is perhaps the most important subskill involved in comprehension (Pressley, 2000). But it's a difficult skill to teach. Unskilled students are prone to say too little or too much in their summaries. GISTing is an excellent strategy for helping students paraphrase and summarize essential information. Students are required to limit the gist of a paragraph to a set number of words. Individual sentences from a paragraph are presented one at a time while students create a gist that must contain only the predetermined number of words. By limiting the total number of words students can use, this approach to summarizing forces them to think about only the most important information in a paragraph, which is the essence of comprehension (Chambliss, 1995).

The first step in teaching GISTing is to select appropriate paragraphs on which to write gists. It's best to start with relatively short paragraphs of no more than three to five sentences that are easily understood. Second, establish a limited number of spaces to represent the total number of words of the gist, say 15 or so. Third, have students read the first sentence of the paragraph and, using only the spaces allowed, write a statement in those spaces, capturing the essential information of the sentence. This is the beginning of their gist. Fourth, have students read the second sentence of the paragraph and, using the information from the first and second sentences of the paragraph, rewrite their gist statement by combining information from the first sentence with information from the second. Again, the students' revised gist statement should be no more than the allotted number of spaces. This process continues with the remaining sentences of the paragraph. As students read each succeeding sentence, they should rework their gist statement by accommodating any new information from the sentence into the existing gist statement, while not using any more than the allotted number of spaces. Finally, students should share their gists for comment and critique.

A social studies teacher taught the GISTing strategy while his class was learning about ancient Rome. He selected a three-sentence paragraph from the textbook to teach gist writing. He began by typing the first sentence of the paragraph on a word processor (using a large font) and projecting it on the screen for his class to see. He then directed students to write a summary of the first sentence using only 15 words. He allowed students to work in pairs. Afterward, he elicited the various first-sentence gists from several pairs of students and projected a version on which the whole class could agree. The teacher and his social studies students went through the same process for the remaining two sentences of the paragraph. As they read the new sentences, they revised their original gist but kept it within the 15-word limit. (See the paragraph and gist sentences below.) By conducting the GISTing lesson with his students, the teacher was able to model and clarify the process throughout, until a final acceptable gist was crafted for the entire paragraph.

Paragraph from social studies text

Julius Caesar was famous as a statesman, a general, and an author, but ancient traffic jams forced him to become a traffic engineer, too. These traffic snarls were so acute in the marketplace of Imperial Rome and around the Circus Maximus that all chariots and ox carts were banned for ten hours after sunrise. Only pedestrians were allowed into the streets and markets. Caesar also found it necessary to abolish downtown parking and establish one-way streets.

Class gist statements for each sentence of paragraph

1. Julius   Caesar   was   famous   for

   many   things   including   traffic   engineer.

   _____   _____   _____   _____   _____

2. As   traffic   engineer,   Julius   Caesar

   banned   chariots   and   ox   carts

   from   Rome   during   the   daytime.

3.

As	traffic	engineer,	Julius	Caesar
banned	all	but	pedestrians	from
Rome	during	the	daytime.	

4.

As	Rome's	traffic	engineer,	Julius
Caesar	allowed	only	pedestrians,	created
one-way	streets,	and	banned	parking.

In this case, technology was used as method for demonstration and for providing an easily viewable model of the process. This illustrates a concept important to technology integration principles: Technology is not thinking. The software will assist in the process, but the thought and learning comes from modeling the appropriate academic tasks, and guiding the students thorough the process until they can produce the gist on their own.

Question-Answer Relationship (QAR)

If every question has an answer, then every answer has a source—that is, the information that supplies the answer. Thus, if we told you there were nearly 2 billion people in China, then later asked you, "What is the population of China?" your answer would be based on the directly stated information we supplied you. If, on the other hand, we asked, "How does China's population compare with that of the United States?" the source of information for answering this second question depends on what you already know about human population statistics of the United States. In other words, the source of information for answering our second question is your prior knowledge.

The QAR strategy teaches students to become sensitive to differing sources of information and, consequently, how to think about what they read and learn at different levels of comprehension (Ezell, Hunsicker, Quinque, & Randolph, 1996; Kintsch, 2005). Students often become conditioned to assume that the answers to any questions will be found directly stated in the material, regardless of the source. This strategy, however, demonstrates for students that at least three sources of information and ideas should be relied on to answer comprehension questions (Raphael & Pearson, 1985). These are:

Right There   Regardless of the information source, the information is directly stated or can be found virtually word for word.

Author & Me   The answer to a question calls for combining information from sources with the students' existing knowledge.

On My Own   Students must rely on what they already know about a topic to answer this type of question.

It helps to contextualize QAR categories by relating them to other ways that levels of processing are characterized. Notice in the following comprehension continuum how *right there* and literal-level thinking about sources of information requires text-based comprehension. In other words, just being able to understand what the text says is enough. On the other end of the continuum is *on my own* and applied-level thinking. This kind of thinking places a heavy demand on what the reader and learner already knows about the topic. In between, readers and learners must combine their prior knowledge with information they glean from sources in order to make meaning.

Comprehension Continuum

Text-Based Comprehension		Learner-Based Comprehension
Literal *Right There*	⇒ Inferential *Author & Me* ⇒	Applied *On My Own*

The best way to understand the thinking involved in QAR is for you to go through the process of identifying sources of information for questions yourself. Read the following short passage, then answer and label the questions that follow it as either *right there*, *author & me*, or *on my own*. We completed the first one for you.

> Today we take transcontinental air travel for granted. To be in New York one morning and the next morning in Beijing is a daily reality for hundreds of business travelers and tourists. Few realize, however, that our first attempts at air flight didn't begin with the Wright brothers in North Carolina 100 years ago, but with the Montgolfier brothers in Paris over 200 years ago. And the first aircraft was not an airplane, but a hot air balloon.

1. Who invented travel by air balloon?

   Answer: the Montgolfier brothers

   QAR Source: author & me

2. Where were the Montgolfier brothers from?

   Answer: _____

   QAR Source: _____

3. Where is Beijing?

   Answer: _____

   QAR Source: _____

Let's analyze these three questions and your responses. Question 1 requires a small inference that connects the final two sentences of the paragraph. Therefore, because the source of information is not stated word for word, we identified it as an *author & me* question. For question 2, the third sentence states nearly verbatim that the Montgolfiers were in Paris, so the source of information needed to answer it is *right there*. Finally, question 3, while alluding to a city named in the paragraph, requires prior knowledge that Beijing is a city in China. Because the text does not provide that fact, the source of information needed *is on my own*.

Teaching students about different levels of processing information and ideas using the QAR strategy begins by familiarizing them with the comprehension descriptors. Teachers have found it helpful to post the *right there, author & me*, and *on my own* labels on chart paper in the room where students can remind themselves that comprehension requires more than word-for-word searching and thinking. The most effective QAR instruction, however, is through teacher modeling and guided practice. Daily reinforcement of *right there, author & me*, and *on my own* comprehension processing will help students internalize higher-level thinking about the sources of information that you make available to them and that they explore on their own.

Technology can assist teachers and students in using the QAR strategy. As will be explored further in subsequent chapters, electronic reading and study systems, and concept mapping software can be used with this strategy.

Process Guides

As students progress through information sources learning about a content area topic, their processing of the information and concepts can be guided. Process guides scaffold students' comprehension within unique formats. They're designed to stimulate students' thinking during or after their reading, listening, or involvement in any content area instruction. Guides also help students focus on important information and ideas, making their reading or listening more efficient (Kintsch, 2005; Kintsch & Kintsch, 2005).

As with the QAR strategy, process guides are designed to move students down the comprehension continuum from

FIGURE 2.5

Process Guide for Archeology

Directions: List the following objects as they were probably found. Place them in correct order on the excavation chart. Be sure to check the "HELP" story for clues. Be prepared to defend your stratification decisions.

HELP!

I am an archeologist. The year is 2050. My team and I discovered a most unusual site. For years, this particular group of humans had deposited objects at a central location. My co-workers did not follow appropriate procedures at a the site. Instead of carefully mapping the area, they just started digging and removing artifacts. Could you help my scientific investigation? If necessary, use the Internet and other classroom resources as guides.

Top Layer: _____

Layer 1: _____

Layer 2: _____

Layer 3: _____

Layer 4: _____

Layer 5: _____

Layer 6: _____

Layer 7: _____

ARTIFACTS

Vacuum tube from a radio

Steering wheel with no horn

Campaign button for LBJ

Cell phone

Beatles' album

Computer keyboard

Wooden buckboard wheel

sentence surfing and repeating back what the text said to connecting information and ideas to prior experience and applying new knowledge (Best, Rowe, Ozuru, & McNamara, 2005). Figure 2.5 presents a process guide that demonstrates this feature admirably. Notice how the statements in the guide for the topic of archeology in a science class stretch students' thinking, pushing them to process new information and ideas at higher levels. Notice, too, the novel and enticing format of the guide. Similar to other content literacy strategies already described, process guides should encourage meaningful thinking while limiting the length of responses. In this way, students are more likely to be motivated to complete them.

Now that you have looked over the process guide for archeology, a few comments are in order. Did you notice that to accomplish the task in the guide, students must be able to think at an applied level about the content? Instead of requiring literal-level processing, the teacher who designed this guide wanted his students to demonstrate that they could do something with their learning about how to investigate archeological sites. Thus, the goals of process guides are to help learners assimilate, think critically about, and apply new knowledge (Caccamise, 2005). Furthermore, the visual nature of the guide makes it ideally suited to a digital presentation on a desktop, laptop, or even a small hand-held screen.

Something else you may have noticed about the process guide is that it forms an excellent basis for class discussion. Once students complete the archeology guide, the science teacher took advantage of its discussion-generation potential. His students challenged each other over several stratification designations, referring to print and digital resources for clarification and confirmation. An important advantage of process guides for teachers is that students must read and think about the information sources rather than skim or scan for answers to text-based questions. In short, students who complete appropriately designed process guides cannot help but to become active learners and higher-level thinkers.

There are no set procedures for creating process guides. The types of guides are as varied as the teachers who construct them. Although guides can take a number of different forms, you must make some important and necessary decisions before designing them:

1. Read the text material thoroughly and decide what information and concepts need to be emphasized.

2. Determine how much assistance your students will need to construct and use meaning at the higher levels of processing. If students already possess a basic understanding of the content, your guides can emphasize higher-level thinking. If, on the other hand, the content is new to your students, then guides might balance text-based and learner-based processing.

3. Ask yourself, "What format will stimulate my students to think about the content in a meaningful and useful fashion, as well as motivate and appeal to them?" In our experience, the more imaginative the guide, the greater the chance that students will complete it. As you'll see in subsequent chapters, technology offers a wide palette of options for creating and presenting process guides.

4. It is critical that students be prepared to use process guides. We recommend that you begin by "walking through" one of the guides, explaining its features, intent, and benefits. Allow students to meet in small groups and complete the guide in class under your supervision and with your assistance. Engage the class in discussion based on their responses to the guide, and use this feedback to provide additional explanation and to make any necessary modifications to the guide. Above all, keep in mind your purpose for using process guides. They should not be used as tests because promoting a right-or-wrong attitude among students undermines the intent—to encourage higher-level comprehension of content area material. It is important, however, that students be responsible for explaining their responses to the guide. Make this an integral part of the process guide activity. Finally, at every opportunity, reinforce the connection between the mental activity required to complete the guides and your expectations of how and what students should be learning.

Word Grids

Another important comprehension process involves learning critical content vocabulary (Nagy & Scott, 2000). Using word grids to teach and learn critical disciplinary terminology is especially helpful because in an organized visual, students record essential vocabulary on one axis of the grid, and major features, characteristics, or important ideas on the other axis. Students fill in the grid, indicating the extent to which the key words possess the stated features or are related to important ideas. Once the grid is completed, students are led to discover both the shared and unique characteristics of the vocabulary words (Johnson & Pearson, 1984). As you'll see in subsequent chapters, because this strategy results in a visual display, it is particularly well suited to computer technology applications.

Figure 2.6 is a word grid created for the study of different computer types. Notice that the vertical axis contains the names of various types of computers, whereas the horizontal axis contains important features or characteristics that help differentiate types of computers. The extra spaces allow students to add more vocabulary and features as they work through the study of the topic.

Teachers can help students construct their own word grid using the table feature of a word processor or a spreadsheet program. To replicate the grid shown in Figure 2.6, begin with a 10 × 10 table in a word processor. Then ask the students to type at the top of the far left column "Computer Types," and in the cells below, type "Analog" and "Digital." Explain to the students that these are the row headings for the two computer types. In the cells next to "Computer Types," direct the students to type the column headings " Measures a Physical Quantity" and "Calculates by Counting." With these entries on their word grids, students then read to learn more about the first two types of computers. They use a 0, 1, and 2 system for linking a computer type listed in the row headings with a description or

FIGURE 2.6

Word Grid for Types of Computers

Computer Types	Measures a physical quantity	Calculates by counting	Fills an entire room	Fits on a desk	Portable	Runs several tasks at the same time
Analog	2	0	1	1	1	1
Digital	0	2	1	1	1	2
Micro	0	2	0	2	2	1
Mainframe	0	2	2	0	0	2
Super	0	2	2	0	0	2

Key   0 = none of the feature; 1 = some of the feature; 2 = all of the feature

feature listed in the column headings. As students read further in their books, access relevant websites, look at digital video clips, and listen to and watch presentations of the topic, they add additional types of computers and additional features, such as "Fills an Entire Room" or "Fits on a Desk." At the conclusion of a couple of lessons on types of computers, students have a word grid completely filled in and ready to be used to prepare for a test (as seen in Figure 2.6). Walking students through the process of deciding on components of the grid and discussing with them the relationship between each major idea and each vocabulary word helps prepare students to generate word grids on their own for learning and study.

In this example, when the grid on computer types was entirely filled in, the teacher explained to her students how they could determine, at a glance, the key characteristics of a particular computer, as well as the similarities and differences between the computers. To reinforce this level of understanding, she asked for information from students related to shared and unique features of the various types of computers, for example: "Name two ways in which micro computers and digital computers are alike" or "Identify two critical differences between analog and digital computers." By involving students in the construction of word grids, the teacher helps students discover how the grid-building process can be applied to the content vocabulary for other topics and in other content areas. Her students are also allowed plenty of time for class discussion and for review of the vocabulary and major ideas. They are given the opportunity to work in cooperative groups where they share their entries on the grids and review each vocabulary word, noting the pattern of numbers they assigned them for each feature.

Strategies That Extend New Learning
RAFT

Once students have acquired new content information and concepts they need opportunities to rework, apply, and extend their understandings. The RAFT writing strategy is uniquely suited to do just that (Santa & Havens, 1995). This form of writing gives students the freedom to project themselves into unique roles and look at content from unique perspectives. From these roles and perspectives, RAFT writing has been used to explain processes, describe a point of view, envision a potential job or assignment, or solve a problem (Fisher & Frey, 2003). It's the kind of writing that when crafted appropriately should be creative *and* informative.

RAFT is an acronym that stands for:

R   Role (role of the writer)
A   Audience (to whom or what the RAFT is being written)
F   Form (the form the writing will take, as in letter, song, etc.)
T   Topic (the subject focus of the writing)

Two different examples of RAFTed assignments are shown in Figure 2.7—one about chromosomes in science and the other focused on whole numbers in math.

FIGURE 2.7

Student Examples of RAFT Writing in Math and Science

R   A whole number between 1 and 9
A   A whole number equal to 10 minus their number
F   A letter
T   Why it's important to be a positive role model for the fractions less than one

Dear Number 7:

It has come to my attention that you are not taking seriously your responsibilities as a role model for the fractions. With this letter I would like to try to convince you of the importance of being a positive role model for the little guys. Some day, with the proper combinations, they too will be whole numbers. It is extremely important for them to understand how to properly carry out the duties of a whole number. For them to learn this, it is imperative for them to have good positive role models to emulate. Without that, our entire numbering system could be in ruins. They must know how to add, subtract, multiply, and divide properly and efficiently. They must know how to respond if ever asked to become a member of a floating point gang. Since they are not yet whole, it is our duty to numberkind to make sure they are brought up properly to the left of the decimal.

Thank you in advance for our support,
The Number 3

FIGURE 2.7

Student Examples of RAFT Writing in Math and Science (continued)

R   Chromosome
A   Daughter chromosomes
F   Letter
T   Cell division during mitosis

Dear Daughter Chromosomes,

You are moving on to better things as part of separate but equal cells. You don't remember me because you are both part of what I was. You see, during Anaphase, I split in two at my centromere. My last minutes were spent with what now accompany you as other daughter chromosomes. Please do not be afraid of the double membrane, called the nuclear envelope, which will soon surround you. It is going to form in order to protect you while you replicate and proceed through what I did. You will eventually split as I did in order to help form another duplicate cell. I write you to wish you luck and share with you my experience so that you may pass it on to others.

Sincerely,
Mr. Chromosome

After covering the topic of the Battle of the Alamo, the teacher conducted a group brainstorm with her class to gather as many possible observers to and players in the events of those fateful days. In this example, using the drawing tools in a word processor, she projected a large oval in the middle of the screen and then used autoshape connectors to add lines and descriptors as students called out responses. (She could have also used a software program that automates the brainstorming process, such as Inspiration.) Eventually, the brainstormed web looked like the one seen in Figure 2.8.

Figure 2.8

Battle of the Alamo Web

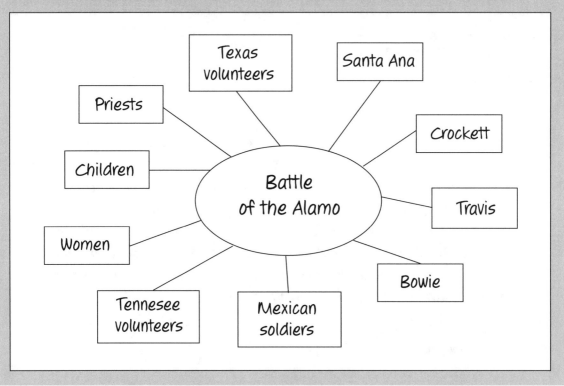

Next, the teacher reviewed the RAFT writing process. For the role of the writer, she asked students to choose one of the perspectives from the web. She then directed the class to write about the major events of the battle from that perspective. This would comprise the topic. With regard to the audience and format, students were given a free choice. One goal with this RAFTed assignment was to provide students a creative format for demonstrating their understanding of the battle. Another goal was to help students' new learning about the Alamo become more permanent as a result of reconsidering the topic then creating a written record in the form of a RAFTed composition. One student wrote from the perspective of a priest in a journal:

San Antonio de Bejar
Sunday, March 6, 1836

There is nothing good here. I am asked to bless this parched earth that runs in streams with the blood of men in blue jackets and animal skins. Santa Ana has me along to make killing justifiable in the eyes of God. But God is on neither side of this carnage.

On this 13th day of the siege, Generalissimo made his assault. After the third attempt on the mission amid a volley of cannonshot and grapeshot on all sides, our soldiers got over the walls. They moved from room to room, fighting all the while for nearly five hours. We were perhaps 1,400 strong to their small garrison. Against my pleading, Santa Ana had the few survivors killed on the spot.

As I walk among the dead in this place of God turned into a house of slaughter, I find the torn and shattered bodies of Crockett, Travis, Bowie, and scores of unknown men, women, and children. Our soldiers are sickened by what they have done. Even Santa Ana desires to leave now and return to Mexico City, but his lieutenants convince him to stay. This means there will be more fighting and bloodshed tomorrow.

Me esculpe, Señor

Julio Escobar

SPAWN

Creating unusual and challenging assignments to stimulate students to extend their understanding of newly learned material is made easier with SPAWN (Martin, Martin, & O'Brien, 1984) prompts. SPAWN stands for *special powers, problem solving, alternative viewpoints, what if,* and *next*; each is a category of writing prompts that can encourage students to move beyond the recall level of thinking (Brozo, 2003). Each category of prompts is explained below:

S *Special Powers*: Students are given the power to change an aspect of the text or topic. When writing, students should include what was changed, why, and the effects of the change.

P *Problem Solving*: Students are asked to write solutions to problems posed or suggested by the books and other sources.

A *Alternative Viewpoints*: Students write about the topics from a unique perspective.

W *What If*: Similar to special powers, the teacher introduces the aspect of the topic that has changed, then asks students to write based on that change.

N *Next:* Students are asked to write in anticipation of what will be covered and discussed next. In their writing, students should explain the logic of what they think will happen next.

For a science unit on the topic of winter, a teacher generated the following SPAWN prompts based on the trade books and other sources the children read:

Special Powers	We have been reading about how snow forms in clouds. You have the power to change that process. What could happen as a result of your change?

Problem Solving	In *Snow Day* the author presents many problems people face when a snowstorm hits their city. Write as many solutions to these problems as you can imagine.
Alternative Viewpoints	We have been learning about how people cope with snowstorms. Tell a snowstorm story as though you were a snowflake.
What If	In *Katy and the Big Snow*, Katy is asked to clear the entire city of snow. What would happen if Katy broke down or got stuck in the snow? When writing, think of how dependent the people of the city of Geoppolis were on Katy's snow-plowing ability.
Next	We have been learning about the effect of global warming on melting glaciers. What do you think will be the next effect of the shrinking ice caps?

These prompts were given to students on different days of the unit. Students wrote responses to them in electronic science logs kept on hand-held computers. These log entries were "beamed" (using the infrared feature) to the teacher's own computer so she could read and respond to them. The science teacher's students enjoyed writing responses to these prompts because they were engaging and could be completed within 10 minutes or so. The SPAWN strategy offers a near endless array of options for focused content writing. Because of the potential variety, SPAWN prompts can be used with any topic and sources, and many other forms of technology. Furthermore, this kind of writing can help provide a more complete picture of students' comprehension and learning.

Reader-Response Writing

The final content literacy strategy we describe is one that makes it possible for students to explore personal connections to information and concepts in the content areas. We read everywhere today and hear from teachers across the country that instructional material must be made relevant to students in order to gain and keep their attention (Bean, 2002). Making learning relevant means linking it to the interests and experiences of learners. When students are invited to find connections between topics in school and their own lifeworlds, they become critical, metacognitive thinkers (Brozo, 1988). They more readily integrate new knowledge into their existing knowledge. And they begin to see a functional utility to learning. Finally, teachers have long known that the more students become personally invested in the content they are reading and studying, the more they will learn.

The reader-response strategy takes students through a questioning-answering process that results in a composition that ties directly to students' attitudes and experience (Petrosky, 1982). Here are three typical reader-response questions:

- What aspect of the topic or text interested you the most?

- How did it make you feel?

- Can you explain your feelings by describing an experience from your own life?

A teacher presented her class with three questions similar to these and asked the students to write a short composition in response. The class had been reading about and studying whales. One student wrote:

> I was most interested in the long trip the gray whales take every year. They travel over 10,000 miles from Alaska to Mexico. I can't believe the whales know where to go every year. They must be really smart.
>
> I feel very small compared to gray whales. If I tried to swim as far as they do it would take me at least 5 years! And I would probably get lost, too.
>
> When I was 7 my family and I drove to the Grand Canyon. It took us three days. It would have taken a lot longer if we had to walk. I tried to help my mom and dad read the map, but it was hard. We got lost a couple of times. I'll bet whales never get lost.

In a health class, the teacher had his students write reader-response essays in response to reading an article titled "Muscles: Use Them or Lose Them." He posed three questions like those you've already seen. A student in his class crafted the following response:

> I thought that the part about resistance exercise can prevent and reverse the effects of the loss of muscle mass in old people was really interesting. As people get older they get weaker, their bones get brittle and their physical condition deteriorates.
>
> It made me feel that I need to keep doing workouts so I don't age as fast. I would like to live to be 100 years old, and be fit at that age.
>
> It made be feel sad, too, because my grandmother broke her hip when she was 62. Her hip never really healed and she had to go to a nursing home. She stopped doing things like picnics and Sunday rides in the car. She didn't do anything but watch TV and sleep. She passed away before her 65th birthday.

Technology applications for content literacy strategies would seem to be limited only by a teacher's creative imagination. In fact, the variety and sophistication of tools in the technology toolkit today can enliven and make more interactive virtually every traditionally mediated literacy strategy. For instance, iPods, de rigueur of most American teens and preteens, can digitally capture a teacher's oral directions for executing a strategy, anticipation guide statements, lesson impression words and phrases, and guiding examples. What's more, downloaded Podcasts can serve as the information source for the readiness strategies presented in this chapter.

Look ahead to Chapters 4 through 7 and review the prototype lessons in social studies, reading, science, and math. Skim through the discussion of technology applications and features listed in Chapter 8. Working with a colleague, suggest potential technology applications for the content literacy strategies over the following topics. We've supplied our own technology suggestions for the first one.

Topic	Content Literacy Strategy
1. Building the great pyramids of Egypt	1. SQPL

Suggested Technology Application: Provide students question starters (e.g., who, what, where, etc.). Use presentation software, with features that include drawing, painting, design, and animation (such as KidPix, Hyperstudio, or PowerPoint) to help them generate their own questions. Hyperlink to websites describing the pyramids to seek answers.

2. The causes of the American Revolution	2. Process guide

Suggested Technology Application: _____

3. Geometric patterns in nature   3. Word grid

Suggested Technology Application: _____

4. An author study of Louis Sacher, author of *Holes*   4. RAFT

Suggested Technology Application: _____

Looking Back

Literacy strategies are essential for promoting thoughtful, engaged, and memorable learning in the content areas. Teachers need to employ effective, evidence-based literacy practices at each phase of a lesson if students are to achieve this level of learning. The strategies and practices described and exemplified in this chapter are based on sound principles and have proven effective for expanding the literacy abilities and disciplinary knowledge of students at virtually every grade level. Their presentation and response formats can be adapted to a range of technology tools that can provide students with a greater variety of supports. Next, we discuss considerations for planning and delivering these strategies.

Questions For Study

- In your capacity as a literacy coach, classroom teacher, or administrator, what are the biggest challenges you and your colleagues face in integrating content literacy strategies into the curriculum? As a team or study group, problem solve how these challenges might be overcome.

- Consider which of the three phases of a content literacy lesson—Readiness, Interactive Comprehension, Extending New Learning—you feel least knowledgeable and skillful. How can you acquire more knowledge and skills in this area? Consult colleagues who can serve as resources for increasing your competence.

- Make one literacy strategy from each of the three phases of a content lesson the focus of study. Find research and professional opinion articles and books about the strategies. Develop a plan for professional development that ensures the strategies become an effective and permanent tool in teachers' instructional toolkits.

References

Bean, T. (2000). Reading in the content areas: Social constructivist dimensions. In M. Kamil, P. Mosenthal, P. D. Pearson, & R. Barr (Eds.), *Handbook of reading research* (Vol. III). Mahwah, NJ: Erlbaum.

Bean, T. W. (2002). Making reading relevant for adolescents. *Educational Leadership, 60,* 34–37.

Beck, I., McKeown, M., Hamilton, R., & Kucan, L. (1997). *Questioning the author: An approach for enhancing student engagement with text.* Newark, NJ: International Reading Association.

Best, R., Rowe., M., Ozuru, Y., & McNamara, D. (2005). Deep-level comprehension of science texts: The role of the reader and the text. *Topics in Language Disorders, 25,* 65–83.

Brozo, W. G. (2005). Connecting with students who are disinterested and inexperienced. *Thinking Classroom/Peremena, 6,* 42–43.

Brozo, W. G. (2004). Gaining and keeping students' attention. *Thinking Classroom/Peremena, 5,* 38–39.

Brozo, W. G. (2003). Writing to learn with SPAWN prompts. *Thinking Classroom/Peremena, 4,* 44–45.

Brozo, W. G. (1988). Applying the reader-response heuristic to expository text. *Journal of Reading, 32,* 140–145.

Brozo, W. G., & Simpson, M. L. (2007). *Content literacy for today's adolescents: Honoring diversity and building competence* (5th ed.). Upper Saddle River, NJ: Merrill/Prentice-Hall.

Caccamise, D. (2005). Theory and pedagogical practices of text comprehension. *Topics in Language Disorders, 25,* 5–20.

Carr, E., & Ogle, D. (1987). K-W-L Plus: A strategy for comprehension and summarization. *Journal of Reading, 30,* 626–631.

Chambliss, M. (1995). Text cues and strategies successful readers use to construct the gist of lengthy written arguments. *Reading Research Quarterly, 30,* 778–807.

Cummins, J. (2001). Magic bullets and the grade 4 slump: Solutions from technology? *NABE News, 25,* 4–6.

Denner, P. R. (2003). The effect of story impressions preview on learning from narrative text. *The Journal of Experimental Education, 71,* 313–332.

Duffelmeyer, R. (1994). Effective Anticipation Guide statements for learning from expository prose. *Journal of Reading, 37,* 452–457.

Duffelmeyer, R., & Baum, D. (1992). The extended Anticipation Guide revisited. *Journal of Reading, 35,* 654–656.

Eccles, J. S., Wigfield, A., Midgley, C., Reaman, D., MacIver, D., & Feldlaufer, H. (1993). Negative effects of traditional middle schools on students motivation. *Elementary School Journal, 93,* 553–573.

Ediger, A., & Pavlik, C. (1999). *Reading connections: Skills and strategies for purposeful reading.* New York: Oxford University Press.

Ezell, H. K., Hunsicker, S. A., Quinque, M. M., & Randolph, E. (1996). Maintenance and generalization of QAR reading comprehension strategies. *Reading Research and Instruction, 36,* 64–81.

Fisher, D., Brozo, W. G., Frey, N., & Ivey, G. (2007). *50 content area strategies for adolescent literacy.* Upper Saddle River, NJ: Merrill/Prentice-Hall.

Fisher, D., & Frey, N. (2003). Writing instruction for struggling adolescent readers: A gradual release model. *Journal of Adolescent & Adult Literacy, 46*, 396–407.

Fisher, D., & Ivey, G. (2005). Literacy and language as learning in content area classes: A departure from "every teacher a teacher of reading." *Action in Teacher Education, 27*, 3–11.

Guthrie, J. T., & Humenick, N. M. (2004). Motivating students to read: Evidence for classroom practices that increase reading motivation and achievement. In P. McCardle & V. Chhabra (Eds.), *The voice of evidence in reading research*. Baltimore: Brookes.

Guthrie J., & Wigfield, A. (2000). Engagement and motivation in reading. In M. Kamil, P. Mosenthal, P. D. Pearson, & R. Barr (Eds.). *Handbook of reading research* (Vol. III). Mahwah, NJ: Erlbaum.

Huffman, L. E. (2000). Spotlighting specifics by combining focus questions with K-W-L. In D. Moore, D. Alvermann, & K. Hinchman (Eds.), *Struggling adolescent readers: A collection of teaching strategies* (pp. 220–222). Newark, DE: International Reading Association.

Hurst, B. (2001). The ABCs of content area lesson planning: Attention to basics, and comprehension. *Journal of Adolescent & Adult Literacy, 44*, 692–693.

Johnson, D. D., & Pearson, P. D. (1984). *Teaching reading vocabulary*. New York: Holt, Rinehart and Winston.

Kintsch, E. (2005). Comprehension theory as a guide for the design of thoughtful questions. *Topics in Language Disorders, 25*, 51–65.

Kintsch, W. (1998). *Comprehension: A paradigm for cognition*. Cambridge: Cambridge University Press.

Kintsch, W., & Kintsch, E. (2005). Comprehension. In S. Paris & S. Stahl (Eds.), *Current issues on reading comprehension and assessment*. Mahwah, NJ: Erlbaum.

Marchand-Martella, N., Wasta, S., & Martella, R. (1996). Applying the K-W-L strategy in health education. *Journal of School Health, 66*, 153–154.

Marshall, N. (1989). Overcoming problems with incorrect prior knowledge: An instructional study. In S. McCormick & J. Zutell (Eds), *Cognitive and social perspectives for literacy and research instruction: Thirty-ninth yearbook of the National Reading Conference* (pp. 323–330). Chicago: National Reading Conference.

Martin, C. E., Martin M. A., & O'Brien, D. (1984). Spawning ideas for writing in the content areas. *Reading World, 11,* 11–15.

McCray, A. D., Vaughn, S., & Neal, L. I. (2001). Not all students learn to read by third grade: Middle school students speak out about their reading disabilities. *Journal of Special Education, 35,* 17–30.

McGinley, W. J., & Denner, P. R. (1987). Story impressions: A pre-reading/writing activity. *Journal of Reading, 31,* 248–253.

Merkley, D. (1996/97). Modified anticipation guide. *The Reading Teacher, 50,* 365–368.

Nagel, K. (1992). *Two crazy pigs.* New York: Cartwheel/Scholastic.

Nagy, W. E., & Scott, J. (2000). Vocabulary processes. In M. Kamil, P. Mosenthal, P. D. Pearson, & R. Barr (Eds.), *Handbook of reading research* (Vol. 3, pp. 269–284). Mahwah, NJ: Erlbaum.

Ogle, D. (1992). KWL in action: Secondary teachers find applications that work. In E. Dishner, T. Bean, J. Readence, & D. Moore (Eds.), *Reading in the content areas: Improving classroom instruction.* Dubuque, IA: Kendall/Hunt.

Petrosky, A. R. (1982). From story to essay: Reading and writing. *College Composition and Communication, 33,* 19–36.

Pressley, M. (2000). What should comprehension instruction be the instruction of? In M. Kamil, P. Mosenthal, P. D. Pearson, & R. Barr (Eds.), *Handbook of reading research* (Vol. III). Mahwah, NJ: Erlbaum.

Raphael, T., & Pearson, P. D. (1985). Increasing students' awareness of sources of information for answering questions. *American Educational Research Journal, 22,* 217–235.

Rosenshine, B., Meister, C., & Chapman, S. (1996). Teaching students to generate questions: A review of the intervention studies. *Review of Educational Research, 66,* 181–221.

Santa, C., & Havens, L. (1995). *Creating independence through student-owned strategies. Project CRISS.* Dubuque, IA: Kendall-Hunt.

Santa, C., & Havens, L. (1991). Learning through writing. In C. Santa & D. Alvermann (Eds.), *Science learning: Processes and applications.* Newark, DE: International Reading Association.

Schmidt, P. R. (1999). KWLQ: Inquiry and literacy learning in science. *The Reading Teacher, 39,* 563–570.

Schunk, D. H., & Zimmerman, B. J. (1998). *Self-regulated learning from teaching to self-reflective practice.* New York: Guilford.

Snow, C. (2002). *Reading for understanding: Toward an R&D program in reading comprehension.* Santa Monica, CA: Rand Education.

Sorcinelli, M., & Elbow, P. (1997). *Writing to learn: Strategies for assigning and responding to writing across the curriculum.* San Francisco: Jossey-Bass.

Strange, T., & Wyant, S. (1999). The great American prairie: An integrated fifth-grade unit. *Social Education, 63,* 216–219.

Sturtevant, E., Boyd, F., Brozo, W. G., Hinchman, K., Alvermann, D., & Moore, D. (2006). *Principled practices for adolescent literacy. A framework for instruction and policy.* Mahwah, NJ: Erlbaum.

White, B., & Johnson, T. S. (2001). We really do mean it: Implementing language arts standard #3 with opinionniares. *The Clearing House, 74,* 119–123.

Wittrock, M. (1990). Generative processes of comprehension. *Educational Pscyhologist, 24,* 345–376.

CHAPTER 3

Designing Lessons to Meet a Wide Range of Abilities

Seeing Forward

The evidence-based content learning strategies just reviewed are tools for developing academic literacy—the reading, writing, speaking, listening, and viewing skills needed to accomplish school-based tasks (Brozo & Simpson, 2007; Fisher & Ivey, 2005). Designing lessons that enable all students to acquire and apply these skills can seem daunting, given the diversity of today's students and increasingly inflexible curriculum and assessment demands. In this chapter we ground the use of content literacy strategies within the framework of Universal Design for Learning (UDL), a way of looking at planning that can maximize the learning potential for all students. A universally designed lesson gives students the flexibility needed to compensate for their learning challenges. Digital tools provide much of this flexibility and support. Designing lessons that combine digital tools with evidence-based literacy strategies can improve learning for all students, but especially for students who struggle (Zorfass, Fideler, Clay, & Brann, 2007).

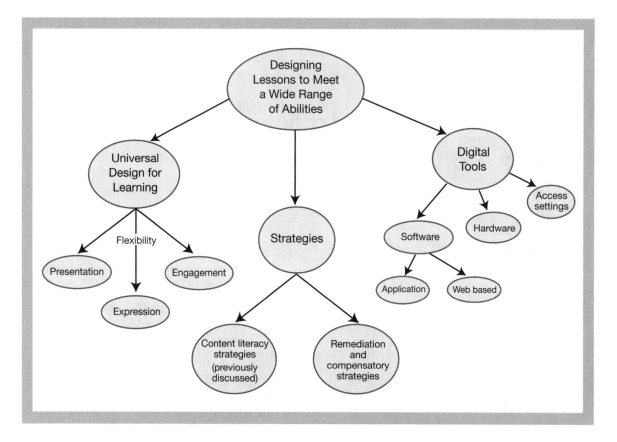

Universal Design for Learning

We ground our examples of lessons that combine reading strategies with appropriate software tools using the concept of Universal Design for Learning (UDL; Rose & Meyer, 2002). Developed by the Center for Applied Special Technology (CAST), UDL is a concept of planning for instruction that accommodates a broad range of learning needs, increasing the probability that all students will be successful. The concept borrows heavily from psychology regarding theoretical constructs about learning and from the field of architecture in addressing issues of access. In a nutshell, the basic concept of UDL is that the learning environment can be designed in a manner that ensures the greatest possible participation. A frequently stated metaphor for UDL is the curb-cut; this simple sidewalk design eliminates a bumpy barrier for individuals who use wheel chairs, and is now viewed as an accommodation needed for mobility and access (Rose & Meyer, 2002). Community planners usually do not retrofit curb-cuts after requests or petitions from individuals who need them; instead, they try to incorporate these features during the initial design phases of the project. They are built in anticipation that someone may need barrier-free mobility, not in response to an identified need. An unintended consequence of the curb-cut design is that others—people pushing baby strollers, or travelers pulling luggage on wheels, or skateboarders—enjoy it and have come to rely on its strategic placement.

The developers of UDL asked the question, What are similar barriers of access to learning in classrooms? Providing students with learning materials and tools that are flexible, that can be changed according to the needs of the learner, is the cornerstone of the UDL framework. Exclusive reliance on print-based materials and paper-and-pencil tasks alone limit participation for students who may not read as fluently or who struggle to write. Digital materials and tools provide this flexibility, allowing the task to be adjustable from the beginning. The UDL framework is an outgrowth of research on three learning networks in the brain: how people recognize concepts, the strategies people use for new learning, and affective concerns—that which motivates people. Three basic principles of UDL support these networks by encouraging flexibility in presentation, expression, and affect.

Principle 1: Support recognition learning by providing multiple, flexible methods of presentation.

This element of UDL encourages teachers to present content using a variety of methods, materials, and sources. Teaching methods that support this principle include providing multiple examples, highlighting critical features, providing multiple media and formats, and supporting background context. Adding digital formats, either in addition to or in place of traditional print-based materials, makes it easier to support recognition learning. Digital images, sounds, and other options can be used as multiple examples to illustrate a concept. Text, if in a digital format, can be read aloud or linked to definitions, other files, or websites that supply background information. These features allow teachers to plan flexibly for students who have difficulty reading or understanding the text. Furthermore, digital examples are much more easily stored, searched, and accessed in the modest space of classrooms and schools than are printed text and hard copy images.

Principle 2: Support strategic learning by providing multiple, flexible methods of expression and apprenticeship.

This element of UDL gives students options for how they will show what they have learned. Teaching methods that support this principle include providing flexible models of what the skill looks like; opportunities to practice with supports and ongoing, relevant feedback; and flexible opportunities for demonstrating the skill. For example, in place of always asking for responses by assigning paper-and-pencil tasks, use technology tools that give students choices in expression formats, such as written, oral, slide show, video, or drawing. Even the word processor, a simple technology innovation that has been around for over a generation, can increase student flexibility of expression by taking the tedium out of editing text and giving support for spelling, grammar, and choice of words.

Principle 3: Support affective learning by providing multiple, flexible options for engagement.

This element of UDL attends to student interest and motivation. Teaching methods that support this principle include offering choices in context, content, and tools. For example, allow the student to select an area of interest in the topic being studied to obtain more information from a variety of sources. Digital formats, whether CD-ROM, websites, or tool-based software, are interactive and engaging. Students enjoy the interest they generate. Most students appreciate the power and the independence that they provide. Other teaching methods that support this principle include offering adjustable levels of challenge to match student interests and skills. For example, the authors of many websites hyperlink important terms to a pop-up screen that offers a definition or more information. This type of support is also available in most electronic text programs; dictionary support is available for the majority of the words in the document and can be accessed with a few mouse clicks. A growing number of online learning materials provide examples of flexible text by providing multiple reading levels, choices in interest area, and multilingual versions (see, for example, StarChild, http://starchild.gsfc .nasa.gov/docs/StarChild/StarChild.html and Windows to the Universe, www.windows.ucar.edu).

Planning for instruction using these three concepts can reduce or eliminate the need to adapt instruction after the fact, saving planning time and making all students feel included. The UDL framework is an evolving concept. There is no one program, set of materials, or method that provides all the elements of UDL. A universally designed curriculum is not available in one set of commercial products. Rather, UDL is a concept for recognizing a variety of learning needs, and providing for those needs. The Center for Applied Special Technology and the National Center on Accessing the General Curriculum have provided emergent examples of these concepts in unit and lesson planning that may be useful for further discussion (Jackson & Harper, 2001).

Digital Tools That Support Universal Design

The digital tools that enable teachers to incorporate UDL principles of flexibility in presentation, expression, and motivation are, for the most part, commonly available in most classrooms. They include application software and web-based applications, hardware, and access settings that can be used to support students as they write, develop presentations, read documents, or access information.

Application Software

Word processors, presentation programs, visual learning software, and electronic reading and study systems are examples of software most commonly found in K–12 environments that can be used to design lessons that support literacy development.

The word processor is the most ubiquitous, adaptable, and useful tool for literacy support. During the last 20 years, it has become more common than typewriters and has made the writing process easier for most people. Those who are poor spellers or inconsistent typists can still produce a letter, a chart, or other documents that are professional looking and error free. The word processor takes the tedium out of revising, editing, and sharpening one's written work.

The same advantages work for students. Word processors can support each phase of the writing process, in prewriting, drafting, editing, and producing the final product. Unfortunately for many students, this tool is overlooked as a routine support; it is more often used as a reward in the final stages of writing process. When used during all phases of writing, word processors support flexible methods of expression and engagement by providing help with spelling, word selection, translation, and grammar, and by supporting the revising and editing process. Standard office-based word processors also have lesser-used features that are often not considered in supporting student expression and engagement. These hidden features, such as voice recognition and executive summaries, allow for greater student independence in accomplishing literacy tasks.

Some students who struggle with academic literacy skills may be able to take advantage of features that are found in specialized word processors. Text-to-speech (TTS) word processors read, or narrate, the text displayed in the document. Word prediction is a feature that suggests a list of intended words from the first few keystrokes, which can provide support for expression for students who have difficulties in transcription, word retrieval, spelling, and fine-motor skills (MacArthur, 1998). Rebus word processors automatically insert a picture above an individual word, which can support flexible student expression and engagement.

Visual learning software offers flexibility in presentation and engagement, bringing the advantages of a digital tool to strategies for text comprehension. These strategies are called a variety of names—idea maps, concept maps, story boards, advanced organizers, webs, or semantic maps. Digital forms of visual learning strategies can be developed using software programs such as Inspiration or Kidspiration (Inspiration, Inc.) or by using the drawing and diagram features on most word processors. When using these digital tools, the display can change in appearance (increasing the size of the screen), in format (having the text read aloud), or in access to further information (using hyperlinks to explanatory files or websites). Teachers can build in these options to support learning differences from the beginning, reducing the need to modify or create alternate assignments or adapt for special learners after the fact (Rose & Meyer, 2002).

Presentation software allows teachers and students to use more than one type of media—text, graphics, audio, animation, and/or video—to communicate a message. PowerPoint (Windows/Mac) and Keynote (Mac only) are the most widely available products, but there are others that were developed for use in school environments, such as Kid Pix Deluxe, HyperStudio, and Intellipics Studio. Video, music, graphics, and text can easily be incorporated into a stand-alone file using Movie Maker or iMovie, programs that are included with most operating systems. Designing lessons that use or develop the multimedia combinations possible through presentation software can increase flexibility in all three areas of UDL—presentation, student engagement, and motivation.

Electronic reading and study systems use text-to-speech technology to read what appears on a computer screen. They also have features that support comprehension strategies, such as highlighting, note taking, bookmarking, and electronic reference. Many also include optical character recognition (OCR) programs that work with a scanner to convert paper-based textbooks to a digital format. These programs increase the flexibility of presentation—away from paper-based text to independently accessed auditory, visual, and interactive accommodations.

Web-Based Applications

Web-based applications allow multiple users to share and collaborate in commenting on, editing, and revising their work. These applications are available to anyone with an Internet connection and a browser. They are based on open-source code that is freely shared, so they do not require purchasing or licensing in order to participate. These web-based applications, known as the Web 2.0, are emerging as useful literacy development tools, especially in areas where collaboration, communication, and creativity are important. The Web 2.0 tools that are basic to educational purposes are blogs, podcasts, and wikis. Other tools include social bookmarking (favorite bookmarks that are stored on a server), photo sharing sites (such as Flickr, www.flickr.com), and video showcasing (such as YouTube, www.youtube.com). Tools once thought of as the domain of the desktop, word processors, spreadsheets, and presentation programs are also included in Web 2.0 applications (Soloman & Schrum, 2007).

Hardware Tools

The software and web-based applications mentioned can be accessed with desktop or laptop computers that are typically equipped—meaning a relatively recent operating system, a CD-ROM, and an Internet connection, preferably high speed. Other hardware that may be needed include a classroom projection system (stationary or touch-interactive), a scanner, and a printer. Although one computer for every student can be thought of as an ideal (or idealized) situation, progress toward technology integration can nevertheless be made with less equipment. Options include setting up as many computer stations as possible for student use throughout the classroom, and frequently scheduling classroom sets of laptop computers (usually stored in a cart that is moved from room to room). Portable word processors, personal digital assistants (often referred to as PDAs or hand-held computers) and digital audio players (such as the iPod) can all function as alternatives to desktop computer access.

Access Tools

Accessibility options modify the monitor display, magnify the screen, or change how the keyboard operates. Most accessibility options are free—built in to operating system software. They make flexible engagement possible for students who have physical challenges, temporary or otherwise. Although these operating system adjustments are sufficient to meet the needs of most students, some students with more significant physical barriers to participation will need accessibility software and device combinations that are more specialized, or dedicated for a particular use. In those cases, assistive technology specialists can help with selection and training of accessibility options.

Balancing Remediation and Compensatory Strategies

The reality of today's schools is often expressed by a great diversity in student achievement—in any given classroom, student skills will vary considerably. Many students still struggle with beginning reading skills, exhibiting limitations in some or all areas of phonetic awareness, decoding, syntax, semantics, or comprehension. Difficulties in reading remain one of the most significant barriers to learning for many students (CAST & LD Online, 2007; Allington, 2002). In the past, the approach to students who were showing these difficulties was remediation, developing fluency in sets of prerequisite skills that had to be mastered prior to advancing to next levels. Remediation strategies, providing additional instructional time and different instructional approaches, are still the most familiar to teachers (Edyburn, 2007). When a student does not know a certain skill—he or she is pulled aside and taught that skill.

But teachers also want these students to understand their textbooks in the subject area, and remediation skill building practices do not always generalize to literacy skills in the content area. Compensatory approaches may also be needed to provide the desired level of performance. Compensatory strategies encourage readers to use an array of supports for understanding the information presented, and for expressing and using that understanding. For students who continue to struggle with content literacy skills, these supports are needed to produce the desired level of performance. Compensatory strategies can be quite simple and "low tech," such as mnemonic phrases written on index cards, or asking a peer or adult to read a portion of text aloud. But even more progress can be made if compensatory strategies are paired with appropriate digital supports, which can be accessed on-demand and independently. Some compensatory strategies have already become part of the general landscape. Spelling and typing errors are caught using auto-correct or notations in word processing; violations of grammar rules are similarly marked. Instead of turning these features off to assess if students can spell accurately on their own (a remediation strategy), teach the students how to use these supports to check and correct their work (a compensatory strategy). Similarly, when reading fluency is less than the demands of the text, in addition to teaching word recognition strategies based on vocabulary from the selection (a remediation strategy), allow students to listen to an audio version using text-to-speech software in order to use the information (a compensatory strategy). When students do not know the meaning of a word, allow them to look it up or to translate it using on-demand electronic resources (a compensatory strategy), rather than waiting to learn the terms before engaging with the text (a remediation strategy).

Must educators decide if the best course of action is remediation or compensation (Edyburn, 2007)? Perhaps this dichotomy produces a false argument. We envision classrooms where teachers are comfortable enough with content literacy strategies and with technology that they are able to incorporate both throughout the curriculum, offering freely accessible supports for those who enjoy them as well as for those who need them. For example, using talking ebooks could support students who are required to understand and use text that is beyond their reading levels. Students who are limited from study by time demands may also take advantage of same supports, listening to text on an iPod in between commutes.

The "yet unimagined literacy" skills needed for the technological world that society is fast becoming demands that students become critical consumers of the information they encounter (IRA, 2001). Remediation strategies alone will not develop these skills. Using compensatory strategies and supports is consistent with the principles of UDL to maximize the potential that all students will be successful by providing flexibility in presentation, engagement, and motivation.

Designing Content Literacy Lessons That Incorporate Technology

The following suggestions will assist in the process of designing content literacy lessons that incorporate technology.

During the initial planning for a unit or a lesson, try to incorporate the three principles of Universal Design for Learning in as many instructional activities as possible.

There are many models for how to plan a unit or a lesson—from direct instruction models, explicit instruction models, and those involving constructivist approaches. However, the important quality, whichever model is used, is attention to as many of the three principles of UDL as possible—flexibility in presentation, expression, and engagement. Not every lesson can incorporate each principle, but analyzing when you are giving students more than one option for receiving, expressing, and engaging with the learning task will maximize your efforts in planning for the successful participation of all students. In addition to CAST's (www.cast.org; Jackson & Harper, 2001) examples of lessons that incorporate UDL principles in unit and lesson planning, the International Society for Technology in Education (ISTE) (www .iste.org) provides lesson plan examples using technology that have been submitted by preservice and inservice teachers across the country. Consider the match of ideas these technology plans describe with the design principles of UDL.

Review the tasks involved in implementing potential content literacy strategies and match these tasks with the salient features of software tools and with your students' instructional needs.

The content strategy and the materials you have to work with should influence the technology you choose for the lesson. The examples provided in subsequent chapters demonstrate text-to-speech, presentation, visual learning software, digital pictures, blogs, and word processing. Use a form of technology appropriate for the task and the students involved. Early elementary students may need more direction and simpler technology (Richardson, 2004).

Remember that technology enhances the learning process; technology is not learning.

The technology is the means for accessing learning. The focus is on the curriculum and learning; technology use per se is not the purpose of the lesson. Technology integration is defined by how and why it is used, not by its amount or type. Use the simplest tool that you are comfortable with (Richardson, 2004). If that solution happens to be a low-technology item (like a sticky note), then don't contrive a technology application to fit.

Technology changes quickly. Make it your personal mission to learn as much about the hardware, software, websites, and social networking sites as appropriate for the ages and subject-area interests of your students.

Become proactive. Learn how the applications presented here can be used to access new learning. Observe student performance and success in using technology, and advocate for needed hardware, software, and services for classroom use.

How does one learn the various software features, and how do you learn to implement them? The International Reading Association (2001) has listed a number of responsibilities for pre-service teacher preparation programs in this area, all designed to develop technology-savvy novice teachers. The IRA position paper on integrating literacy and technology in the curriculum suggests that inservice teachers take full advantage of professional development opportunities. Stay current on the research on practical ideas for using technology by exploring strategies and resources developed by others through professional electronic mailing lists, as well as professional publications such as books and print and online journals.

THINK and APPLY

1. Take the opportunity to explore further the concepts presented here. Visit CAST's website: www.cast.org. How did UDL evolve? From links on the homepage, explore CAST's development of WiggleWorks and the Thinking Reader. How can these products inform your own lesson design process? Choose the link *Articles about UDL* and read one article of interest. Bookmark these locations on your own computer and make notes on your perceptions.

2. Learn more about IRA's position on literacy and technology by reading *Integrating Literacy and Technology in the Curriculum* retrieved from www.reading.org/downloads/positions/ps1048_technology.pdf. How might you work with your colleagues to achieve the vision proposed in this paper?

Looking Back

There is much work to do. Students are exposed to an online world where anyone can print or produce anything, without conventional societal constraints for veracity or point of view. The adults we are training as students now will need to be able to critique information developed in a variety of formats, developed from points of view that are not always transparent. These students already have skills in accessing an array of technology tools—cell phones, text messaging, social networking sites—that can be harnessed for literacy development. Yet, even though the students possess or easily generalize technology skills, schools have lagged behind in their efforts to integrate technology into regular classroom practice. For example, the IRA position statement on integrating reading and technology in the curriculum criticizes the fact that not one state allows the use of the word processor in writing assessments, and all states have ignored all but paper-and-pencil tasks in their assessment of reading abilities. And although professional organizations that are devoted to technology integration (such as ISTE) list planning for technology as skills in their standards for teachers, the practice has not yet been realized. When it comes to using technology as part of pedagogy, many teachers are either occasional or nonusers (Cuban, Kirkpatrick, & Keck, 2001). Hopefully, highlighting the work of researchers in the areas of literacy, technology, and universal and instructional design will demonstrate possibilities in literacy development that are indeed "as yet unimagined" (IRA, 2001).

In the following chapters we pair literacy strategies with technology features and put them together in prototypical lessons in social studies, reading and language arts, science, and math. The following chart previews the content literacy strategy, a technology application, and the UDL principles each lesson supports. We hope that you will be able to take these ideas and put them to use in different contexts and for different purposes, while retaining the basic aspiration of maximizing success for all learners.

Content Area	Content Literacy Strategies	Digital Tools	General UDL Features: Flexibility in 1 = Presentation, 2 = Expression 3 = Engagement
Social Studies			
Readiness	SQPL	Visual learning software	1, 2
Interactive comprehension	Process Guide	Word processor, electronic reading and study system	1, 3
Extending new learning	SPAWN	Presentation software	1, 2, 3
Reading and Language Arts			
Readiness	KWL	Visual learning software	1, 3
Interactive comprehension	GISTing	Presentation software, word processing, blogs	1, 2, 3
Extending new learning	RAFT	Word processing, presentation software	1, 2, 3
Science			
Readiness	Anticipation Guide	Word processing	1, 2
Interactive comprehension	QAR	Word processing, visual learning software	1, 2
Extending new learning	Reader-Response Writing	Presentation	2, 3
Math			
Readiness	Lesson Impressions	Blogs, visual learning software, presentation software	1, 2, 3
Interactive comprehension	Word Grid	Word processing, electronic reading and study systems	1
Extending new learning	RAFT	Word processing, presentation	2, 3

Questions for Study

- Individually or as a group or committee, analyze elements of the current curriculum. Are there places where flexibility in presentation and/or student expression could be included or improved on? What resources would be necessary to integrate these principles?

- Individually or in small groups, access NASA's site for students (StarChild, http://starchild.gsfc.nasa.gov/docs/StarChild/StarChild.html). Compare the content and wording between levels 1 and 2 of this site, and then explore the advanced level. What elements of universal design for learning do you recognize in this site? What design elements are the most completely developed? How might you apply these design principles to content that you are teaching?

References

Allington, R. L. (2002). You can't learn much from books you can't read. *Educational Leadership, 60*(3), 16–19.

Brozo, W. G., & Simpson, M. L. (2007). *Content literacy for today's adolescents: Honoring diversity and building competence* (5th ed.). Upper Saddle River, NJ: Merrill/Prentice-Hall.

Center for Applied Special Technology & LD OnLine (2007). *An educator's guide to making textbooks accessible and usable for students with learning disabilities.* Retrieved September 27, 2007, from www.ldonline.org/article/16310.

Cuban, L., Kirkpatrick, H., & Peck C. (2001). High access and low use of technologies in high school classrooms: Explaining an apparent paradox. *American Educational Research Journal, 38*(4), 813–834.

Edyburn, D. (2007, January/February/March). Technology-enhanced reading performance: Defining a research agenda. *Reading Research Quarterly, 42*(1), 146–152.

Fisher, D., & Ivey, G. (2005). Literacy and language as learning in content area classes: A departure from "every teacher a teacher of reading." *Action in Teacher Education, 27*, 3–11.

Hall, T., Strangman, N., & Meyer, A. (2003). *Differentiated instruction and implications for UDL implementation.* Wakefield, MA: National

Center on Accessing the General Curriculum. Retrieved May 14, 2008, from www.cast.org/publications/ncac/ncac_diffinstructudl.html.

International Reading Association. (2001). *Integrating literacy and technology in the curriculum.* Retrieved September 30, 2007 from www.reading.org/downloads/positions/ps1048_technology.pdf.

Jackson, R., & Harper, K. (2001). *Teacher planning and the Universal Design for Learning environments.* Peabody, MA: Center for Applied Special Technology. Retrieved September 30, 2007, from www.cast.org/publications/ncac/ncac_teacherplanning.html.

MacArthur, C. A. (1998, Spring). Word processing with speech synthesis and word prediction: Effects on the dialogue journal writing of students with learning disabilities. *Learning Disability Quarterly, 21* (2) 155–166.

Richardson, J. (2004, July/August). Content area literacy lesssons go high tech. *Reading Online, 8*(1). Retrieved September 30, 2007, from www.readingonline.org/articles/art_index.asp?HREF=richardson/index.html.

Rose, D., & Meyer, A. (2002). *Teaching every student in the digital age.* Retrieved September 27, 2007, from www.cast.org/teachingeverystudent.

Solomon, G., & Schrum, L. (2007). *Web 2.0 new tools, new schools.* Eugene OR: International Society for Technology in Education.

Strangman, N., Hall, T., & Meyer, A. (2003). *Graphic organizers with UDL.* Wakefield, MA: National Center on Accessing the General Curriculum. Retrieved September 30, 2007, from www.cast.org/publications/ncac/ncac_goudl.html.

Zorfass, J., Fideler, E., Clay, K., & Brann, A. (2007, May). Enhancing content titeracy: Software tools help struggling students. *Technology in Action, 2*(6), 1–12.

Social Studies:
Content Literacy and Technology

Seeing Forward

Thus far, we have made the case based on policy, research, and practical knowledge for the integration of technology and content literacy into the instructional routines of classroom teachers. In this chapter and the three to follow, we present actual specific content examples of how technology integration can occur. This chapter is devoted to demonstrating numerous ways content literacy strategies for social studies learning can be supported and extended through the use of technology tools. A lesson focus and content literacy strategies from the three primary phases of a quality lesson—readiness, interactive comprehension, and extending new learning—are presented. With technology applications, these strategies become even more interactive and engaging to young learners from across the ability spectrum. What's more, the information and ideas gleaned from this chapter will provide teachers of social studies and other content material the tools for creating their own technology-mediated content literacy lessons.

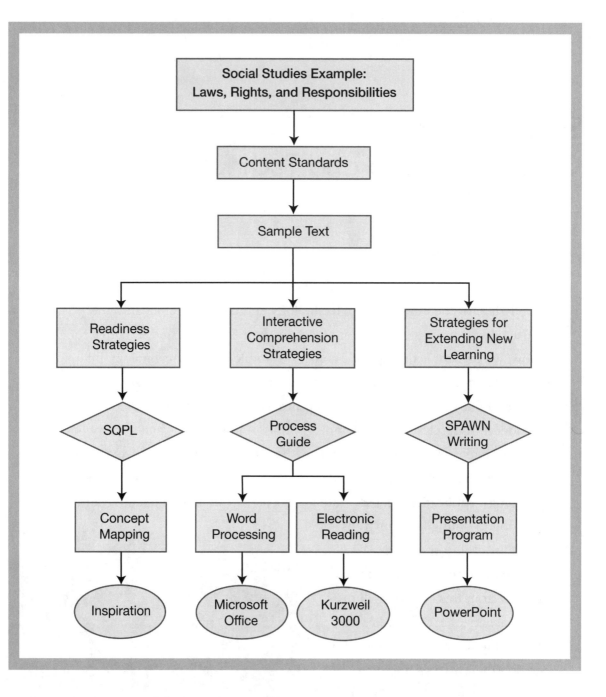

Teacher: Mrs. Fuentes
Grade level: Fourth
Lesson topic: Laws, Rights, and Responsibilities

Content Standards

Content standards applicable to this lesson are:

- *Identify the purpose and importance of a rule or a law.*

- *Describe the significance of the Declaration of Independence, the U.S. Constitution, and the Bill of Rights (e.g., basic freedoms).*

- *Identify the rights and responsibilities of citizenship in making the nation a better place to live.*

Sample Text for This Lesson

The United States Constitution

The United States Constitution is made up of three main sections. First, there is the Preamble, which doesn't describe any rights but explains the reasons for the Constitution. Next are the Articles of the Constitution. There are seven articles that describe the system of government, the powers of the different branches of government, and the process of making laws. The third section of the Constitution is the Amendments or the Bill of Rights. The Amendments are laws that protect the rights of citizens to enjoy certain freedoms, but also responsibilities to uphold those freedoms.

The Bill of Rights

The Bill of Rights was passed because some people were afraid that the government would have too much power. These people were afraid that some important things could be made illegal, and they wanted to be sure to keep those things legal.

Soon, the new government started meeting. Congress proposed the Bill of Rights. A list of 12 changes was sent to the states. In 1791, 10 of those changes were agreed to by the states.

The 10 changes were added to the Constitution. These 10 changes are called the "Bill of Rights."

A bill of rights is a list of rights that belong to the people. The government is not allowed to break these rights. Some of these rights might sound familiar: the right of free speech, the right to practice your own religion, the right to be silent if you are arrested. The original Constitution had no bill of rights. Many of the framers of the Constitution did not think it was needed. But many people wanted one, so promises were made to add one. Once the new government was running, a bill of rights would be added.

The Bill of Rights makes it possible for you to say whatever you want about the President of the United States. You can say that you don't like his hair. You can say that you don't like his voice. You can say that you don't like his policies regarding the war in Iraq. You can say that you don't like his tax ideas. It seems normal to Americans to be able to say these things. We can criticize the president. We can criticize a member of Congress. We can criticize a mayor. We can say what things they do that we don't like. This is only possible because of the right of free speech. The Bill of Rights protects free speech.

Imagine if there was no right to free speech. A law could be passed that says that if you criticize the president's hair, you can spend a day in jail. Or worse, criticizing the president's taxes can get you a year in jail. These are the kinds of laws that the framers of the Constitution were afraid of. The Bill of Rights protects us from such laws. We cannot be put in jail because of our opinions.

First Amendment to the Constitution

This is what the First Amendment says in the Bill of Rights:

> Congress shall make no law respecting an establishment of religion, or prohibiting the free exercise thereof; or abridging the freedom of speech, or of the press; or the right of the people peaceably to assemble, and to petition the Government for a redress of grievances.

The First Amendment includes the rights many Americans hold most dear, and it forms the foundation of American democratic government. The five freedoms listed in the First Amendment—religion, speech, press, assembly, and petition—make it so people, like you and me, can govern ourselves. Without the freedoms in the First Amendment, it would be impossible for Americans to have any other rights. Thus, the First Amendment is the most important amendment in the Bill of Rights.

Freedom of Speech and Press

The Constitution *does* protect the freedom of speech of every citizen. It even protects noncitizens' rights to free speech. This protection is only from the government of the United States and individual states. There are plenty of other places where your right to free speech is not protected. There is no restriction on freedom to speak where you work. For example, your boss can tell you not to talk freely about politics, about religion, about legal issues, even about the latest TV show. Freedoms of speech that apply to the government do not apply to private persons or workplaces. For another example, the government cannot ban any newspaper because that would be taking away the right of the free press. However, the owner of a newsstand does not have to sell every newspaper.

Readiness

Strategy: Student Questions for Purposeful Learning (SQPL)

Technology Application

One computer with concept mapping software and a computer projection system (either a data projector or an interactive whiteboard).

Software Used in This Lesson: Inspiration

Recall that the SQPL strategy, introduced in Chapter 2, asks the teacher to present the students with a question-provoking statement related to the topic they are about to study. For this lesson, Mrs. Fuentes introduces the topic of rights, laws, and responsibilities by projecting the following statement on the whiteboard:

The U.S. Constitution gives you the right to freely surf the Internet.

Mrs. Fuentes used a concept mapping program called *Inspiration* to conduct the strategy with various technology applications. To begin, she opened a new document in Inspiration. A new diagram opens with a main idea symbol highlighted. She typed the thought-provoking statement in its place, adds and links an additional symbol with the text "Our questions about this statement" (a similar statement may be used). This screen was then displayed to her students with an invitation to them to suggest ways to personalize the symbols from the symbol library. As you can see in Figure 4.1, Mrs. Fuentes' fourth-graders changed the symbols to include a drawing of the U.S. Constitution and a light bulb. These symbols are included in Inspiration's extensive symbol library.

Next, Mrs. Fuentes instructed her students to work in small groups to generate two to five questions they would like to have answered based on the thought-provoking statement. She rotated around the room as groups brainstormed questions, offering clarification and monitoring student progress. When the groups finished their questions, Mrs. Fuentes began an interactive discussion with the class, eliciting and displaying questions generated from each group in the concept map. Common or similar questions were regarded as class consensus questions and were given priority. Mrs. Fuentes noticed a couple of important questions had not been asked, so she invited students to "whisper" additional questions. As several students began whispering questions to her, she added her own important questions to the concept map and gave credit to the class for helping think of "these outstanding additional questions." The key here was for Mrs. Fuentes to encourage discussion around the questions with her students, and to make a display of the questions available to the whole class. Here are some of the important questions the students generated. Note how they are displayed in the concept map.

Sample Student Questions

1. Where does it say this in the Constitution?
2. What other rights are there in the Constitution?
3. Does the Constitution give me the right to buy any toy I want?
4. Does the Constitution give rights to kids my age?
5. Does the Constitution only talk about rights?

After the questions were generated and discussed, Mrs. Fuentes had her students engage with the lesson content. Students read excerpts and sections related to the relevant sections of the U.S. Constitution from their textbook, listened to Mrs. Fuentes explain and elaborate, and discussed issues and examples. Her students worked independently and in small groups, focusing on and writing answers to the questions. The following are sample answers her students derived for questions 1 and 5.

1. The Constitution doesn't say anything about the Internet but gives everyone freedom of speech in the Bill of Rights. This means I can look at anything I want to on the Internet. In some countries, like North Korea, people can go only to certain places on the Internet. The government controls what they can see and read.

5. The Constitution talks about more than just rights. It also talks about responsibilities. Everyone is responsible for following the rules of the Constitution. Like if someone is accused of committing a crime, we are responsible to give him a fair trial.

Once the answers were developed, Mrs. Fuentes placed them in the Inspiration file. In Figure 4.1, the answers to questions 1 and 5 were entered using the note feature. Notes have a control that allows them to be shown or hidden—a feature that is useful for display or for study skill development.

Inspiration software automatically generated for Mrs. Fuentes and her class an outline of the concept map, as shown below. She and her students added further material and notes to this outline to assist in the writing process, and also printed it to generate individual study notes. This outline was saved in a format that could be used by word processors.

> The U.S. Constitution gives you the right to freely surf the Internet.
>
> I. Our questions about this statement
>   A. Where does it say this in the Constitution? The Constitution doesn't say anything about the Internet but gives everyone freedom of speech in the Bill of Rights. This means I can look at anything I want to on the Internet. In some countries, like North Korea, people can go only to certain places on the Internet. The government controls what they can see and read.
>   B. What other rights are there in the Constitution?
>   C. Does the Constitution give me the right to buy any toy I want?
>   D. Does the Constitution give rights to kids my age?
>   E. Does the Constitution only talk about rights? The Constitution talks about more than just rights. It also talks about responsibilities. Everyone is responsible for following the rules of the Constitution. Like if someone is accused of committing a crime, we are responsible to give him a fair trial.

Figure 4.1

Student Questions for Purposeful Learning: Concept Map

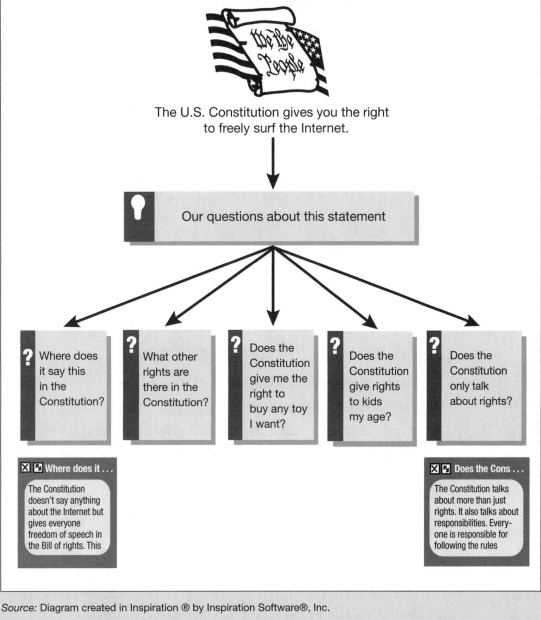

The U.S. Constitution gives you the right to freely surf the Internet.

Our questions about this statement

? Where does it say this in the Constitution?

? What other rights are there in the Constitution?

? Does the Constitution give me the right to buy any toy I want?

? Does the Constitution give rights to kids my age?

? Does the Constitution only talk about rights?

☒ ↩ Where does it . . .

The Constitution doesn't say anything about the Internet but gives everyone freedom of speech in the Bill of rights. This

☒ ↩ Does the Cons . . .

The Constitution talks about more than just rights. It also talks about responsibilities. Everyone is responsible for following the rules

Source: Diagram created in Inspiration ® by Inspiration Software®, Inc.

<table>
<tr><td>

TIPS

- A quick way to input the symbols with links for the questions is to use the "rapid fire" feature of the program. See Inspiration documentation for more details.

- This example assumes the teacher is using one computer and a projection system for all students to see. In classrooms equipped with multiple computers or individual laptops, students may input their own answers and notes in the concept map.

- Inspiration has developed additional software that enables the program to be used on emerging technologies, such as portable word processors and hand-held devices.

- Inspiration software contains features to help students with disabilities use the software. These features include screen magnification, changing the size and color of the symbols and text, keyboard shortcuts, and a talking interface. The software also supports operating system accessibility options, such as sticky keys and mouse keys.

</td></tr>
</table>

Interactive Comprehension

Strategy: Process Guide

Technology Application

Word processing using the following features: templates, forms, and embedded Internet links. Multiple computer stations that can be used with small groups or individually (laptops or hand-held computers). An example of using electronic reading and study program to support the text and the completion of the guide is also presented.

Software Used in This Lesson: Microsoft Office XP, Kurzweil 3000 Process guides use questions and activities to stimulate thinking and focus attention on critical vocabulary, information, and concepts, thereby guiding the exploration of a topic. Process guides also afford a great opportunity to use some of the advanced features of word-processing programs. These features help structure the task for the student.

A process guide Mrs. Fuentes designed for this lesson is seen in Figure 4.2. Note that the guide is a series of three activities that balance text-based and learner-based processing. In many ways, it looks very much like a typical paper-based worksheet created on a word processor. However, the teacher's guide also uses features of a word processor to structure spaces for answers and explanations, to launch web-based activities, and to assist her in creating engaging activities. This process guide uses three major features: form fields, hyperlinks, and templates.

Form Fields: Have you ever tried typing a response into the underlined blank spaces that were created on a word-processed form? The lines seem to "grow" as you type, and unless you go back to underline the response, the area looks uneven. To avoid this, Mrs. Fuentes added form fields to the process guide, as she does with any other form or worksheet, which gave the student a specific and neat place for responses. In Microsoft Word (XP), Mrs. Fuentes located this feature under view>toolbars>forms. She inserted a text form field from this smaller forms toolbar. The text form field can be formatted to specify any number of characters in the answer—and the default is unlimited.

Hyperlinks: The Internet can be a powerful resource and learning tool. However, time and safety concerns may prevent some teachers from utilizing this valuable resource in their classrooms. Free surfing and unsupervised use is risky and can create frustration among students. Furthermore, students can invest a great deal of time in Internet searching and obtain too few resources that are a good match for their topics and questions, or too many hits of questionable value. Even though her school district uses filtering systems that prevent objectionable or unsafe content from being seen, Mrs. Fuentes knows how to create an even safer environment without compromising interest. She directs her students toward child-friendly search engines such as Yahooligans, or specifies predetermined URLs for them to view. In her process guide for laws, rights, and responsibilities, predetermined URLs are embedded in the document in the form of hyperlinks, which launch a browser to open specific websites. These URLs were obtained using a number of search engines (e.g., www.google.com, www.yahooligans.com, or www.ask.com) and searchable sites such as Kathy Schrock's Guide for Educators (http://school.discovery.com/schrockguide/). In this case, Mrs. Fuentes copied and pasted the URLs into the document. She also made it possible for hyperlinks to other documents, programs, and websites to be added through the insert menu on the toolbar (insert>hyperlink>link to).

Templates: Document templates are used by a number of professionals who must supply specific information within a standard format, such as legal documents, psychological reports, and medical reports. Mrs. Fuentes knows that using a document template assures that she will retain the original, unanswered version of the process guide without the risk of overwriting. Once she completed the process guide, she chose "save as" from the menu. In the "save as" type box, she clicked "Document Template." She paid close attention to the location stated in the "save in" box where the template was to be saved—the default location is the Templates folder—and switched to a subfolder in the documents file for saving. She then gave this document template file a different name from the original. When the student opened the document template, it was automatically titled "Document 1" (or another number if other files are open). The students were directed to provide a unique name during the save process, so as to leave the original document intact.

FIGURE 4.2

Process Guide for Laws, Rights, and Responsibilities

Directions: The purpose of this guide is to help you better understand the topic of Laws, Rights, and Responsibilities. Read the suggestions and answer the questions using information and ideas from the book and from class activities.

1. Begin by reading the chapter on Laws, Rights, and Responsibilities. Pay close attention to the first paragraph, which summarizes the contents of the United States Constitution.

   What are the three main parts of the U.S. Constitution?

   1. _____

   2. _____

   3. _____

2. Now, find the words *rights* and *responsibilities* in the text. Also listen closely to the explanation and examples I give for these two important terms. Use the following online dictionaries to explore the meanings of these terms and find more information. Remember, you can access these sites from a word processor by using control>click on the link.

   ■ The Merriam-Webster online dictionary is accessed at www.m-w.com/dictionary/

   ■ This site gives the choice of a variety of dictionary choices: www.onelook.com

   ■ This site leads to Wiktionary, an online dictionary that also gives translations of the chosen word into numerous languages: http://en.wiktionary.org/wiki/Main_Page

   Write a short definition of these terms and give an example from your own life:

   Rights

   Definition: _____

   _____

   Example: _____

   _____

   Responsibilities

   Definition: _____

   _____

   Example: _____

   _____

FIGURE 4.2

Process Guide for Laws, Rights, and Responsibilities (continued)

3. Using any of the Internet sites provided, look up information about the first right in the Bill of Rights that gives people freedom of speech. Try to find out why the founders of our country wanted to make freedom of speech the first right.

- Ben's guide to U.S. Government for Kids: http://bensguide.gpo.gov/index.html

- A brief history of the Bill of Rights: www.freedomforum.org/packages/first/Curricula/ EducationforFreedom/BriefHistory.htm

- The United States Bill of Rights, from Wikipedia, a free encyclopedia: http://en.wikipedia .org/wiki/United_States_Bill_of_Rights

- Constitution Fast Facts: www.constitutioncenter.org/explore/FastFacts/index.shtml

- Text of the first amendment, with an explanation from the National Constitution Center: www.constitutioncenter.org/constitution/details_explanation.php?link=120&const=08_amd_01

- Help rebuild the "missing" Bill of Rights document in an interactive game: http://www .constitutioncenter.org/kidinteractive/final.html

After exploring these sites, explain why the founders of our country wanted to make freedom of speech the first right. Write your explanation here:

_____

_____

TIPS

- When developing a process guide, use "tables" to help organize information.

- Microsoft Word has a built-in speech-to-text feature that transforms spoken words into text. Using this feature is not automatic—it requires the user to "train" the voice recognition files ahead of time, and its accuracy is influenced by the quality of the microphone and the background noise in the room. However, some students may find this feature to be a novel approach and therefore motivating; students with writing disabilities may find it to be an essential adaptation.

- Remind students to use the automatic spell and grammar check features of the word processor, correcting errors as they compose their answers and explanations. Since a process guide is not used as a test or an assessment, we recommend that students be reminded to apply these features. When using a word processor in other activities, such as assessment, these features can be deactivated.

- If the process guide is to be displayed using a computer projection system, be sure to increase the size of the view. Twelve-point font size is very difficult to read from a projection screen. Try adjusting the projected size using the zoom feature of the word processor (view>zoom>zoom to). If the choices presented there are not adequate, consider increasing the font size in the display document.

- Some students may need more writing support than that which is offered through a standard word processor. Consider adapting this assignment using text-to-speech word processors such as Intellitalk (Intellitools, Inc.) or Write:Outloud (Don Johnston).

Using Electronic Reading Support

Mrs. Fuentes's process guide shown in Figure 4.2 was used with a variety of text-based sources. For her students whose reading fluency or word recognition skills are such that reading the text would be laborious, she employed electronic reading support with the print content of this lesson. Electronic reading support usually involves running a software program that reads the text aloud to the student. Further enhancements, depending on features of the particular software program, include dictionary support, note taking, highlighting, and extracting sections of text for further review.

The first step Mrs. Fuentes took in providing electronic reading support for her weaker readers was to get the text into a digital format. This was accomplished in a number of ways. First, she manually converted the paper image of the text into digital text so that it could be displayed on the computer screen. The paper image was converted to text by using a scanner and an OCR, or optical character recognition, software program. Examples of programs that use OCR to convert printed text are electronic reading and study (ERS) programs, such as Kurzweil 3000 and Read and Write Gold. Mrs. Fuentes used Kurzweil 3000 OCR software. This program, and other similar OCR programs, automatically converts text and reads it aloud with a choice of voices and speeds. The programs offer additional reading support, such as dictionary, thesaurus, highlighting, note taking, and extracting segments of text to a new document.

Mrs. Fuentes likes electronic reading and study programs because they are the easiest to use and offer the most additional features. They are also more expensive. In the event that these programs are not available, there are other ways that the teacher, or the student, could convert the paper text to digital text. A standard version of optical character recognition software, such as *Omni Page*, is usually included with most scanners. These programs will scan the document and convert it into digital text. The next step, getting the document to a point where the text can be read, involves copying this text, then pasting it into a text reader program, such as Read Please (a free or shareware program); a text-to-speech word processor, such as Intellitalk or Read:Out Loud, or, for younger students, a rebus-based word processor such as Picture it. The text could also be pasted into current versions of Microsoft Word, either the Windows or Mac version. These programs have text-to-speech capabilities, but they do not highlight text as it is read, nor are they as user-friendly as other programs for younger students.

The second way to obtain a digitized version of the reading selection is to locate the text in the format of a NIMAS-ready file. NIMAS, the National Instructional Materials Accessibility Standard, is a standard format that can be readily converted to alternate format—such as Braille or text to speech. The NIMAS file is not user-ready; it must be opened using a software program that supports this format, such as those listed above. Obtaining the reading selection in NIMAS format eliminates the need to scan the document. Currently, this format is obtainable from the National Instructional Materials Accessibility Center (www.nimac .us). While these services are currently available only for students who qualify as print disabled, the instructional materials market is quickly developing in a way that makes it possible for districts to purchase accessible versions for all students who could benefit. These services may not be currently available in your district, but they are likely to be within the next few years.

Mrs. Fuentes converted the printed text section using Kurzweil 3000 (see Figure 4.3). Once converted, the program will read the text aloud, highlighting each sentence and word as it progresses to give an additional visual cue. In this text segment, the words *rights* and *responsibilities* have also been highlighted, and the first two questions from the process guide have been added to the text. Mrs. Fuentes's student used an electronic dictionary, accessed by selecting a word and clicking on the definition tool. The Kurzweil 3000 was also used to read text found in the Internet activities listed in the process guide. This program accepted both a paper-based and file-based version of the actual process guide, and the student typed responses directly on this document—for further electronic reading and writing supports.

Extending New Learning

Strategy: SPAWN Writing

Technology Application

Presentation program using hyperlinks and voice recording. This lesson was designed for use with one computer equipped with a projection system (either a data projector or an interactive whiteboard).

Software Used in This Lesson: Microsoft PowerPoint

Mrs. Fuentes knows that SPAWN is a simple yet powerful strategy for extending learning. Recall, from Chapter 2, that this strategy

FIGURE 4.3

Example of Text Converted into a Digital Format

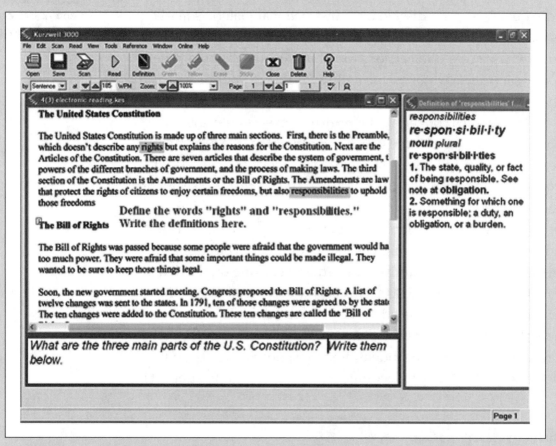

Source: Material created using Kurzweil 3000® by Kurzweil Education Systems, Inc. Used with the permission of Kurzweil Education Systems, Inc.

uses writing prompts to encourage students to move beyond the recall level of thinking. SPAWN is an acronym for the prompts "Special powers," "Problem solving," "Alternate Viewpoints," "What if," and "Next." Mrs. Fuentes gave these prompts to students regularly throughout the study of the topic, and students were directed to write short responses from the viewpoint presented. The example in Figure 4.4 illustrates how the teacher used the prompt "Special powers" with technology applications. She also

FIGURE 4.4

Example of SPAWN Prompts Displayed in an Electronic Presentation Program

SPAWN	SPAWN Challenge: Special Powers
■ Today, your SPAWN challenge is Special Powers. ■ To prepare for your special powers, view an overview of first amendment rights. ■ 1Voice: Know your rights	A group of students who are not in favor of the war in Iraq wear black armbands to school. The principal tries to force students to take the armbands off. He says there is a school rule against it. The students refuse and are expelled from school. The students' parents take the case before a judge.
SPAWN Challenge Special Powers ■ You are the judge in the case. ■ How would you rule and why? ■ What effect would your ruling have on the freedom of speech rights of students?	If desired, plan to place student repsonses on the next group of slides, as shown next.

used two highly recommended websites that helped her students extend the learning from the text. *1voice: Know Your Rights* is a 3-minute video that provides an overview of first amendment rights, and *1Voice: School Uniforms* is a 3-minute video that explores the question of whether school uniforms and dress codes infringe on the right to free speech. Although adding a video clip is not "officially" part of the SPAWN strategy, Mrs. Fuentes did that for this lesson to generate interest and to reinforce what had been read and discussed up to that point about laws, rights, and responsibilities. These particular clips may be found at http://www.channelone .com.

Sample Prompt: Special Powers: A group of students who are not in favor of the war in Iraq wear black armbands to school. The principal tries to force students to take the armbands off. He says there is a school rule against it. The students refuse and are expelled from school. The students' parents take the case before a judge.

You are the judge in the case. How would you rule and why? What effect would your ruling have on freedom of speech rights of students?

We would expect an appropriate student response for this prompt to be similar to the following, written by a student whom we shall call Donovan.

> If I were the judge in this case I would allow the students to wear the armbands. Even though students aren't adults, they have rights too. Wearing armbands is the way the students are saying they do not like the war. That means it's like speech. The Constitution says all of us have freedom of speech. So the students should be free to say they're against the war by wearing the armbands. If the students were allowed back to school with the armbands, other students would feel free to express their feelings about the war. Some might want to say they are in favor of the war. That would be okay too.

In this lesson, Mrs. Fuentes used a presentation program, such as Microsoft PowerPoint, to present the prompt to her students. PowerPoint is easy to use and is ubiquitous—that is, readily available on most computers. Mrs. Fuentes knew that two PowerPoint features would fit well with this strategy: hyperlinks and voice recording.

PowerPoint, like many other software programs, uses hyperlinks to launch a browser and display a predetermined website. In the first slide of the teacher's lesson, notice that she inserted a hyperlink to a video clip residing on the Web. Rather than displaying the entire URL for this clip, she used the name of the clip, *1Voice: Know Your Rights*, as the "text to display." (Find this command under insert>hyperlink and insert the URL.)

The second slide displays the situation, described by Mrs. Fuentes as a "SPAWN Challenge." The third slide gives the students the special powers of a judge and directs them to decide the dispute and to explain the reasons for the decision. Notice that the SPAWN Challenge spans two slides. This was designed purposefully for ease of reading. Mrs. Fuentes tried not to add too much text to a slide or work in a font that was too small to view comfortably. The standard 12-point font, used as a default in word-processing documents, is much too small to be projected.

After showing the video clip and explaining the task, students developed a short description of how they would rule on the armband case, and gave their reasons why. Mrs. Fuentes's classroom was ideal in that students had access to laptops, portable computers, hand-held computers, and shared computer stations to complete their responses. Classrooms that are not as well equipped with technology will adapt accordingly—after all, the graphite pencil and paper have been a standby for generations.

Mrs. Fuentes wanted the students' finished responses to be added to the slide show. In Figure 4.5, Donovan's response is displayed. Here, he added a recording (located at insert>movies and sounds>record sound) to further explain his ruling. This feature was used by Donovan and other students who have difficulty expressing themselves in writing and who prefer to prerecord their presentations. This also made the assignment more interesting and engaging for Donovan and his classmates.

Finally, after all the "Special powers" were gathered, Mrs. Fuentes showed the video clip *1Voice: School Uniforms* (see Figure 4.6). In this clip, other students across the country expressed their opinions on school dress codes, including controversies regarding armbands and other unusual clothing. Mrs. Fuentes's students were invited to compare their ruling with that of other students in the video clip. This final video clip was not a required

FIGURE 4.5

Example of a Student Response Using the SPAWN Strategy

Our Special Powers

- If I were the judge in this case I would allow the students to wear the armbands. Even though students aren't adults, they have rights too. Wearing armbands is a way the students are saying they do not like the war. That means it's like speech. So the students should befree to say they're against the war by wearing the armbands. If the students were allowed back to school with the armbands, other students would feel free to exress their feeling about the war. Some might want o say they are in favor of the war. That would be okay too.

- Donovan's ruling: 🎧

FIGURE 4.6

SPAWN Comparison Prompt

Other Opinions

- You had the special power to make a decision on armbands.

- How does your decision compare to the decisions of other students?

- View the 3-minute video that explores the question of whether school uniforms and dress codes infringe on the right to free speech.

- 1Voice: School Uniforms

element of the SPAWN strategy, but was added for interest and to further stimulate discussion regarding her students' understanding of first amendment rights.

TIPS

- Be careful not to overload the slides with text or to make the font size too small for viewing.
- Personalize the PowerPoint presentation with meaningful graphics, colors, and backgrounds. The slides in this example were left intentionally void of color and pictures for the sake of clarity.
- When using voice recording options on a number of slides, monitor the resulting file size. It may be better to split the presentation files into two or three files, with hyperlinks between them, than to have a file size that is too big to effectively move or email.
- The video clips in this example do not have a closed captioning feature. Use clips that have closed captioning whenever possible.

Looking Back

In this chapter you discovered many ways technology tools can be used to enhance and give energy to content literacy strategies. As we know, student motivation often increases when given alternative modes of presentation and expression made possible through the kinds of technology applications described in this chapter, such as Inspiration, Kurzweil, and versatile word-processing templates. Furthermore, adapting strategy presentation and response modes offers students with diverse abilities easier accessibility to content learning. Although laws, rights, and responsibilities from social studies was the content focus in this chapter, the literacy strategies and technology applications described and exemplified can be used with virtually any content in social studies and in other subject areas. In the next chapter, which focuses on English/language arts, we present additional ways that technology tools can be linked with content literacy strategies to increase motivation and learning for all students.

Question for Study

■ It is important to appreciate that Mrs. Fuentes's knowledge of
and skills with technology and content literacy did not develop
overnight. It took dedication, time, and support to reach her
level of expertise. Consider the kind of commitment to technology and content literacy you and your colleagues would need
to make in order to arrive at a similar level of expertise as Mrs.
Fuentes. With your colleagues, map out an action plan to do so
with the following components:

Goals and Objectives: What do you and your colleagues want
to achieve in terms of technology and content literacy in your
classroom/school?

Actions and Enactors: What will get done and by whom to
achieve your goals and objectives for technology and content
literacy?

Timeline: When will critical actions related to a technology/con-
tent literacy plan get done?

Outcomes: How will you and your colleagues determine if your
actions met the goals and objectives related to technology and
content literacy?

Resources: What supports will be needed to achieve the expected
outcomes for a technology/content literacy plan developed by
you and your colleagues?

CHAPTER 5

Language Arts:
Content Literacy and Technology

Seeing Forward

In Chapter 4 you were introduced to Mrs. Fuentes' fourth-graders and their use of various types of technology tools for learning about laws, rights, and responsibilities in the United States Constitution. In this chapter we offer another classroom envisionment of creative technology applications for each of the three phases of a content literacy lesson focused on the study of heroes and heroines for English/Language Arts. As the teacher, Mrs. Williams, demonstrates, programs such as Kidspiration, Inspiration, and the versatile information formatting capabilities built into Word programs can be exploited to increase motivation for learning, elevate levels of thinking, and increase retention of content.

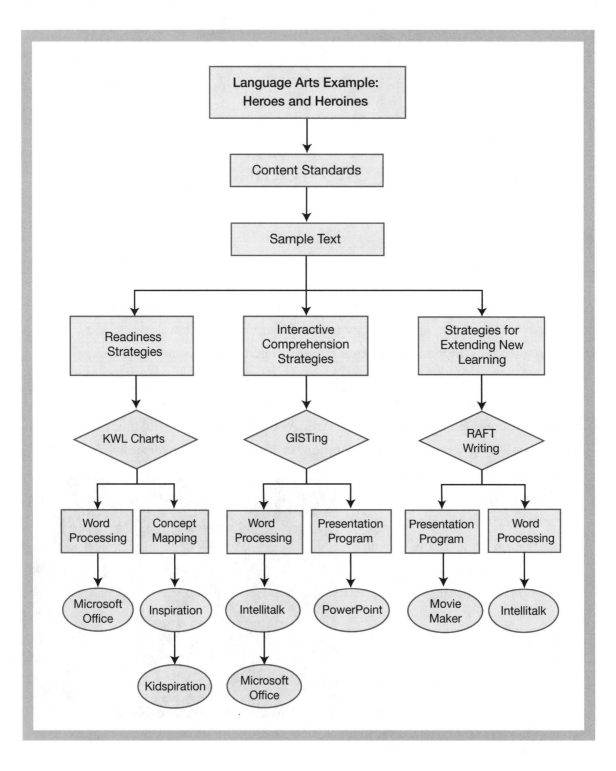

Classroom Case Study

Teacher: Mrs. Williams
Grade Level: Fifth
Lesson Topic: Heroes and Heroines

Content Standards

Content standards applicable to this lesson are:

- Identify cultural characteristics—including customs, traditions, and viewpoints—found in national, world, and multicultural literature in oral and written responses.

- Demonstrate understanding of information in grade-appropriate texts using a variety of strategies, including summarizing and paraphrasing information.

- Write for various purposes, including explanations of stories and poems using retellings, examples, and text-based evidence.

Sample Text for This Lesson

Heroes and Heroines

In mythology and folklore, a hero (male) or heroine (female) usually behaves in ways that are considered good and noble in that culture. Typically the willingness to sacrifice the self for the greater good is seen as the most important defining characteristic of a hero or heroine.

The word *hero* or *heroine* is sometimes used to describe the main character of a story, even if the character does not display heroic behavior. In modern movies, the hero is often simply an ordinary person in extraordinary circumstances. Despite the odds being stacked against him or her, the person succeeds in the end. In some movies (especially action movies), the hero may exhibit characteristics such as superhuman strength and endurance. Often a hero in these situations has a villain. The hero must overcome the villain's attempts to destroy him or her.

Sometimes a person will behave in courageous ways and achieve a high status in people's minds. This often leads to myths about the person. Myths are stories that describe people or gods with extraordinary powers acting in superhuman ways. Myths can develop about real people.

Sometimes we create heroes when times are very hard. For example, during the Great Depression in the United States in the 1930s, many real and made-up heroes were born. For some people, President Franklin Roosevelt was a hero, because he helped them through the hard times. When this happens, a hero becomes a role model to whom others can look for strength and hope.

Readiness

Strategy: KWL Charts
Technology Applications

An electronic concept mapping program or a word processor can be used with this strategy. In order to develop the content of the KWL charts with the students, one computer and a computer projection system (either a data projector or an interactive white board) is needed. After the initial phases of the KWL chart are developed, the teacher may use multiple computer stations that can be used with small groups or one-to-one computing with laptops or hand-held computers.

Software Used in This Lesson: Inspiration, Kidspiration, Microsoft Office

As explained in Chapter 2, a *KWL* chart stands for (1) what I already *know (K)* about the topic; (2) what I *want (W)* to know about the topic, expressed in the form of questions; and (3) what I *learned (L)* about the topic and what I found after answering the questions. The KWL strategy is used to activate prior knowledge and to elicit questions from students before reading and learning.

Mrs. Williams's lesson involved asking students first to generate a list of what they already know about the topic of heroes and heroines and then questions they would like answered as they read and explore information on the topic. She prompted students to think of what they already know based on the following questions:

- What is hero? What would someone have to do to be considered a hero?

- Can a girl or woman be a hero? What do we call a female hero?

- What do you already know about heroes and heroines?

The fifth-graders were asked to write what they already know in the first column of the KWL chart. Then, as the students progressed through the lesson, they identified answers to the questions they generated about the topic in readiness.

To begin the lesson on heroes and heroines, Mrs. Williams used the software program Inspiration to develop a simple KWL chart. Basic shapes (in Figure 5.1 she used rectangles called "process blocks") were positioned and sized on the screen to form the structure for the chart. The chart was saved as a template before any content was added, in order to preserve the format for other topical activities. Mrs. Williams knows that classroom lighting, preferences, and interest levels of her students can dictate color or fill patterns within the display, but for clarity she presented students with a chart on a white background.

Mrs. Williams projected the chart for the entire class to see, and conducted a discussion session in which the chart was filled in based on contributions from her students. She used the preceding questioning prompts to guide the students as they supplied statements describing what they already knew about the topic and questions they wanted answered as they read and explored the content. These statements and questions were typed into the "Know" or "Want to Know" boxes as they were being offered and discussed.

Figure 5.1

Chart for Heroes

HEROES		
What I Know	**What I Want to Know**	**What I Learned**
Heroes do something brave. Heroes make other people feel better. A hero rescues someone. A hero doesn't have to be someone famous. People look up to heroes. A heroine is a female hero.	• Can a hero or heroine be like a mom or dad? • Who were famous heroes and heroines of the past? • Who are heroes of today? • What did they do to become heroes and heroines?	

Source: Diagram created in Inspiration ® by Inspiration Software®, Inc.

Once Mrs. Williams entered statements and ideas in the concept map using the *Inspiration* program, they could easily be transformed into other formats. This same transformation is possible with similar concept mapping programs. In Figure 5.2, the KWL chart is displayed in outline format. It may be printed as is and used as a note-taking guide, or exported to a word processor and opened on group computer stations, laptops, or hand-held computers.

FIGURE 5.2

Heroes KWL Chart in Outline View

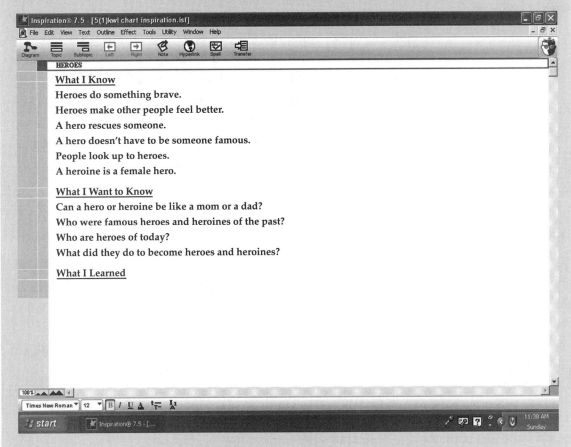

Source: Diagram created in Inspiration® by Inspiration Software®, Inc.

The final step in the KWL chart process, after reading and exploring the topic, is to revisit the chart to answer the questions and add additional information. Once the chart was completed, Mrs. Williams displayed it for students using a data projector; however, other means, such as paper or electronic file, are common display options.

Kidspiration, which is Inspiration Inc.'s concept mapping program for students in grades K–5, offers a predesigned KWL chart template, which Mrs. Williams used to develop another display of the "Heroes" information (see Figure 5.3). This template uses the "super grouper" feature, a large area where pictures and words that categorize a concept may be placed. She added three "super grouper" starburst shapes at the bottom of each KWL category on the template, so that students could add more pictures of heroes from the extensive picture library within the program as well as digital images from other sources. Mrs. Williams conducted this activity in a manner similar to the procedures she used for the KWL template, with group discussions to determine what was known, wanted, and learned.

TIPS

If you do not have access to electronic concept mapping programs, a simple word-processor application also works well with this strategy. A KWL chart can be developed in a variety of ways. The easiest is to compose a 3-column, 2-row chart. In the first row, state the titles ("What I know," "What I want to know," "What I learned"). Then, begin typing content in the first column, second row. The chart will expand with each line entered—as a result of text entry or by pressing the "enter" key. The KWL chart will then be filled in, used and revisited in the same manner described above.

What I **Know**	What I **Want** to Know	What I **Learned**
■ Heroes do something brave. ■ Heroes make other people feel better. ■ A hero rescues someone. ■ A hero doesn't have to be someone famous. ■ People look up to heroes. ■ A heroine is a female hero.	■ Can a hero or heroine be like a mom or a dad? ■ Who were famous heroes and heroines of the past? ■ Who are heroes of today? ■ What did they do to become heroes and heroines?	

Figure 5.3

Heroes KWL Chart

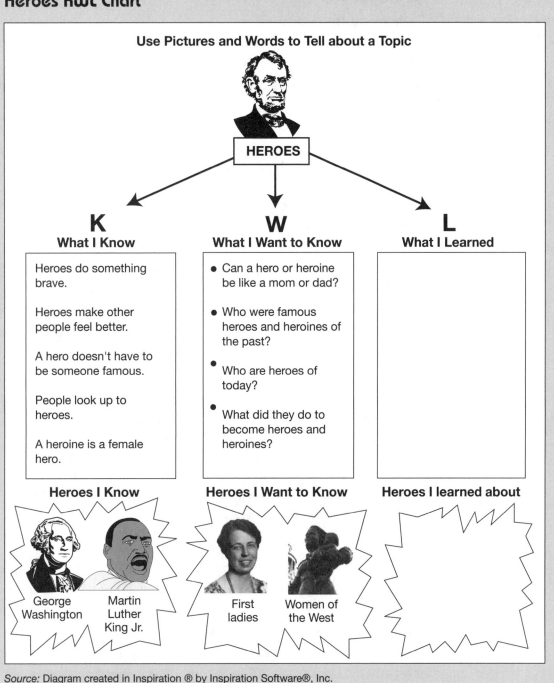

Use Pictures and Words to Tell about a Topic

HEROES

K
What I Know

Heroes do something brave.

Heroes make other people feel better.

A hero doesn't have to be someone famous.

People look up to heroes.

A heroine is a female hero.

W
What I Want to Know

- Can a hero or heroine be like a mom or dad?

- Who were famous heroes and heroines of the past?

- Who are heroes of today?

- What did they do to become heroes and heroines?

L
What I Learned

Heroes I Know

George Washington

Martin Luther King Jr.

Heroes I Want to Know

First ladies

Women of the West

Heroes I learned about

Source: Diagram created in Inspiration ® by Inspiration Software®, Inc.

Interactive Comprehension

Strategy: GISTing

Technology Applications

A presentation program, such as PowerPoint, for the initial teaching phase of the strategy, with word processing used during independent practice. In order to develop initial gists with the students, one computer and a computer projection system (either a data projector or an interactive whiteboard) is needed. Students develop their own gists using word processing on laptops, computers in a lab, or hand-helds, or in small or rotating groups at computer stations.

Software Used in This Example: Microsoft PowerPoint, Microsoft Word, Intellitalk

Recall from Chapter 2 that in GISTing, students write a summary sentence or gist of a paragraph using a limited number of words. A gist is written for the first sentence, revised for the next, and so on, until key information and ideas from every sentence in the paragraph is incorporated into the gist. Consider the possibilities with this passage:

> What we like in heroes today we liked in heroes many years ago. Most of us think of people like Abraham Lincoln or Joan of Arc when we hear the word *hero*. These are people who did big, important things. But we also see heroism in the things that people close to us do everyday. For example, most of us say our hero is a friend or a mother or father.

For purposes of classroom discussion, in which Mrs. Williams and the class developed the gists together, PowerPoint was an excellent display tool. She set up the display for the gist by placing the entire paragraph on the first slide, the first sentence on the next slide, sentences 2 and 3 on the third slide, and so on. Mrs. Williams took advantages of using PowerPoint over general word process-

FIGURE 5.4

GISTing

GISTing What we like in heroes today we liked in heroes many years ago. Most of us think of people like Abraham Lincoln or Joan of Arc when we hear the word *hero*. These are people who did big important things. But we also see heroism in the things that people close to us do everyday. For example, most of us say our hero is a friend or a mother or father.	What we like in heroes today we liked in heroes many years ago. ■ Gist for sentence 1:
What we like in heroes today we liked in heroes many years ago. Most of us think of people like Abraham Lincoln or Joan of Arc when we hear the word *hero*. ■ Gist for sentences 1 and 2:	What we like in heroes today we liked in heroes many years ago. Most of us think of people like Abraham Lincoln or Joan of Arc when we hear the word *hero*. These are people who did big important things. ■ Gist for sentences 1, 2, and 3:

ing as a display feature because of its ability to add pictures or sound, change to interesting backgrounds, and keep the display in a type size that is easier to view when projected. Other presentation programs, such as Hyperstudio, Kidpix plus, or Intellipics Studio, could be used in a similar manner. Through discussion, Mrs. Williams and her students developed the gist for sentence 1, and placed it on the slide, then worked through the procedure with each new sentence. The PowerPoint file looked like Figure 5.4.

Once the idea of a gist was firm with her students, Mrs. Williams developed independent practice exercises using a word processor. Figure 5.5 shows Mrs. Williams's template for the

GISTing strategy using Microsoft Word. The content of this file is an outline that breaks down the structure of the strategy in a step-by-step manner. The template was developed with the intent that it be used in a one-to-one computing situation, either with computers in a lab or with hand-held computers. Note that the directions ask the students to use certain word processing features within the context of an authentic task. Rather than retyping the completed sentence, students were directed to copy and paste the previous sentence, and then change, or edit it, to include the new information. Similarly, the word count feature was used to determine the sentence length. Mrs. Williams also encouraged the students to use other supports that make learning word-processing skills worthwhile, such as grammar and spell checks, and accessing synonyms for a particular word (heroism has no less than 8 suggestions for alternate words).

Alternatives when equipment is scarce or not available would be to have students work in pairs or teams at computer stations. The teacher may also add the paragraph to be gisted to the template and print it for the students to use as a paper-and-pencil worksheet. If printed versions are used, change the directions to eliminate the word-processing skills and add blanks to the document to structure the writing space. Figure 5.6 shows a partially completed GISTing template created by Mrs. Williams.

Mrs. Williams knew that her students would need additional practice with this strategy in order to feel comfortable summarizing text. Therefore, she took advantage of electronic books—one source for selecting text to use in practicing the GISTing strategy. A favorite source for Mrs. Williams is The Electronic Text Center (http://etext.lib.virginia.edu), with its extensive database of literature that is easily accessed in an electronic format. These texts are freely available for noncommercial use, provided the source is given. Most are classic pieces of literature that are no longer restricted through copyright. Mrs. Williams used this etext source to further develop her students' GISTing capabilities. The

FIGURE 5.5

GISTing Template

GISTing

When we put something that we read into our own words, it is called a *gist*. Let's practice gisting, which is putting what we read into our own words.

Write the gist of this paragraph, using the step-by-step directions below.

Type the paragraph to be gisted here.

Write each gist sentence using no more than 12 words. Count the words, or highlight the sentence and go to "tools>word count" to have the computer count them for you.

1. Read the sentence below. Write gist sentence 1 so that these ideas are in your own words.

   1. Copy and paste the first sentence of the paragraph here.

Compose gist sentence 1 and type it below.

Gist sentence 1:

2. Copy and paste gist sentence 1 to the space for gist sentence 2. Then read the new sentence below. Change gist sentence 2 so that it combines the ideas from sentence 1 with this new sentence.

   2. Copy and paste the second sentence of the paragraph here.

Gist sentence 2:

3. Copy and paste gist sentence 2 to the space for gist sentence 3. Then read the new sentence below. Change gist sentence 3 so that it combines the ideas from sentences 1 and 2 with this new sentence.

   3. Copy and paste the third sentence of the paragraph here.

Gist sentence 3:

4. Copy and paste gist sentence 3 to the space for gist sentence 4. Then read the new sentence below. Change gist sentence 4 so that it combines the ideas from sentences 1, 2, and 3 with this new sentence.

   4. Copy and paste the fourth sentence of the paragraph here.

Gist sentence 4:

5. Copy and paste gist sentence 4 to the space for gist sentence 5. Then read the new sentence below. Change gist sentence 5 so that it combines the ideas from sentence 1, 2, 3, and 4 with this new sentence.

   5. Copy and paste the fifth sentence of the paragraph here.

Gist sentence 5:

FIGURE 5.6

Partially Completed GISTing Template

GISTing

When we put something that we read into our own words, it is called a *gist*. Let's practice gisting, which is putting what we read into our own words.

Write the gist of this paragraph, using the step-by-step directions below.

> *What we like in heroes today we liked in heroes many years ago.*
> *Most of us think of people like Abraham Lincoln or Joan of Arc when we hear the word* hero.
> *These are people who did big, important things.*
> *But we also see heroism in the things that people close to us do everyday.*
> *For example, most of us say our hero is a friend or a mother or father.*

Write each gist sentence using no more than 12 words. Count the words, or highlight the sentence and go to "tools>word count" to have the computer count them for you.

1. Read the sentence below. Write gist sentence 1 so that these ideas are in your own words.

   1. What we like in heroes today we liked in heroes many years ago.

Compose gist sentence 1 and type it below.

Gist sentence 1:
> *Heroes today are the same as they were in the past.*

2. Copy and paste gist sentence 1 to the space for gist sentence 2. Then read the new sentence below. Change gist sentence 2 so that it combines the ideas from sentence 1 with this new sentence.

   2. Most of us think of people like Abraham Lincoln or Joan of Arc when we hear the word hero.

Gist sentence 2:

3. Copy and paste gist sentence 2 to the space for gist sentence 3. Then read the new sentence below. Change gist sentence 3 so that it combines the ideas from sentences 1 and 2 with this new sentence.

   3. These are people who did big, important things.

Gist sentence 3:

4. Copy and paste gist sentence 3 to the space for gist sentence 4. Then read the new sentence below. Change gist sentence 4 so that it combines the ideas from sentences 1, 2, and 3 with this new sentence.

   4. But we also see heroism in the things that people close to us do everyday.

Gist sentence 4:

FIGURE 5.6

Partially Completed GISTing Template (continued)

5. Copy and paste gist sentence 4 to the space for gist sentence 5. Then read the new sentence below. Change gist sentence 5 so that it combines the ideas from sentence 1, 2, 3, and 4 with this new sentence.

   5. *For example, most of us say our hero is a friend or a mother or father.*

Gist sentence 5:

example shown in Figure 5.7 was developed by copying a portion of the web-based text (in this case, the opening paragraph) from *Rebecca of Sunnybrook Farm*, by Kate Douglas Wiggin, to a word-processing document. Mrs. Williams used standard tools of highlighting and inserting a text box to develop this GISTing activity. Students had immediate access to the text to be summarized and typed the sentences associated with the strategy directly into the text box. Since Mrs. Williams's students were already familiar with the GISTing strategy, instructions were not provided regarding combining sentences and keeping to a certain length. Those instructions could be added elsewhere on the page if needed.

For her struggling learners, Mrs. Williams offered additional needed supports to help them learn how to summarize using the GISTing strategy. One such support was a text-to-speech word-processing program called Intellitalk for students in need of more structure. In Figure 5.8 you can see how the teacher used the same template structure offered in the "Heroes" example and added further support features unique to most text-to-speech software. Note the addition of blank lines for the gist sentences. These are answer fields, a feature of the program that accepts new text in designated areas only and allows the remaining text

FIGURE 5.7

Example Using Public Domain Electronic Books with the GISTing Strategy

The old stage coach was rumbling along the dusty road that runs from Maplewood to Riverboro. The day was as warm as midsummer, though it was only the middle of May, and Mr. Jeremiah Cobb was favoring the horses as much as possible, yet never losing sight of the fact that he carried the mail. The hills were many, and the reins lay loosely in his hands as he lolled back in his seat and extended one foot and leg luxuriously over the dashboard. His brimmed hat of worn felt was well pulled over his eyes, and he revolved a quid of tobacco in his left cheek. There was one passenger in the coach—a small dark-haired person in a glossy buff calico dress. She was so slender and so stiffly starched that she slid from space to space on the leather cushions, though she braced herself against the middle seat with her feet and extended her cotton-gloved hands on each side, in order to maintain some sort of balance.

Gisting sentences for the highlighted text:

1. An old stage coach was traveling on a dusty road.

2. Jeremiah's stage coach carried the mail slowly along a hot, dusty road.

3.

4.

to be locked. Note also the grouping of seven words at the bottom of the screen (same, saying, said, say, says, sat, sale). This is a display of the word prediction feature (accessed by clicking on the "crystal ball" on the toolbar). In this case, the desired word, *same*, is displayed as choice number 1. The student had the option to click on the word to place it in the answer field, or to continue typing the full word with this model. Word prediction is a useful feature for students who have difficulty thinking of the "next" word, or who are labored in their typing. The words that are "predicted" within a document may be customized, with vocabulary terms pertinent to the lesson added.

The final step in GISTing is for the students to share their gists for comments and critique. There are a number of technology applications that could be used:

FIGURE 5.8

GISTing Strategy Using a Text-to-Speech Word Processor

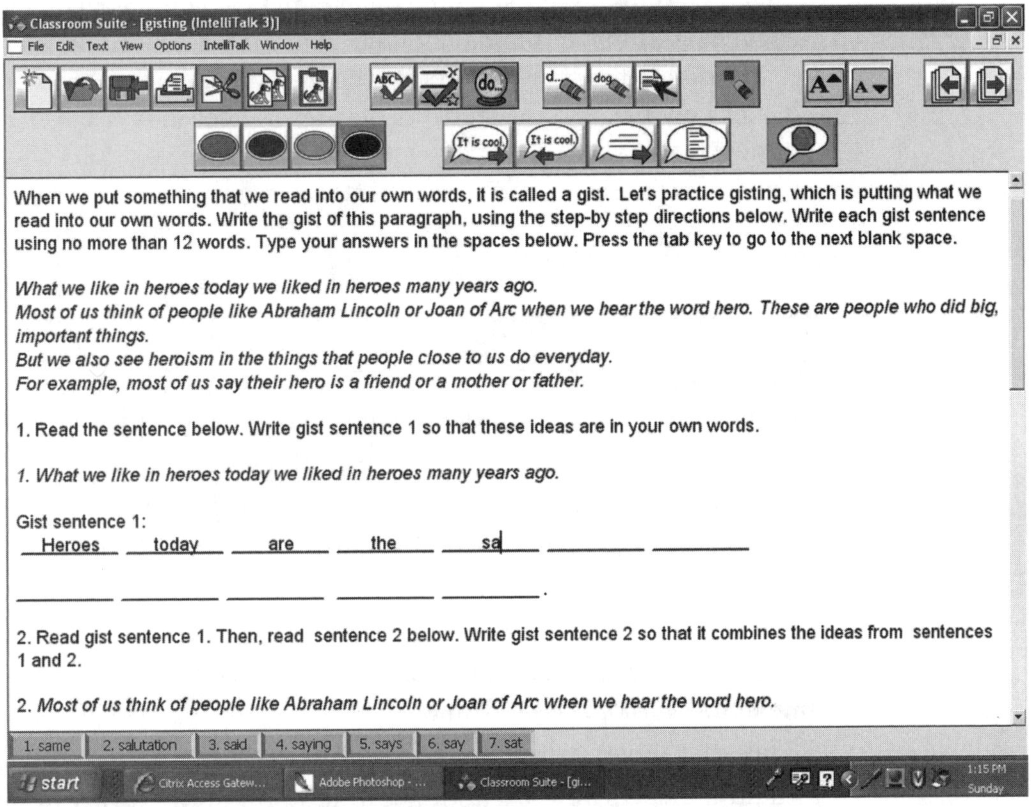

Classroom Suite - [gisting (IntelliTalk 3)]

File Edit Text View Options IntelliTalk Window Help

When we put something that we read into our own words, it is called a gist. Let's practice gisting, which is putting what we read into our own words. Write the gist of this paragraph, using the step-by step directions below. Write each gist sentence using no more than 12 words. Type your answers in the spaces below. Press the tab key to go to the next blank space.

What we like in heroes today we liked in heroes many years ago.
Most of us think of people like Abraham Lincoln or Joan of Arc when we hear the word hero. These are people who did big, important things.
But we also see heroism in the things that people close to us do everyday.
For example, most of us say their hero is a friend or a mother or father.

1. Read the sentence below. Write gist sentence 1 so that these ideas are in your own words.

1. *What we like in heroes today we liked in heroes many years ago.*

Gist sentence 1:
Heroes   today   are   the   sa_____ _____ _____

_____ _____ _____ _____ _____ .

2. Read gist sentence 1. Then, read sentence 2 below. Write gist sentence 2 so that it combines the ideas from sentences 1 and 2.

2. *Most of us think of people like Abraham Lincoln or Joan of Arc when we hear the word hero.*

1. same | 2. salutation | 3. said | 4. saying | 5. says | 6. say | 7. sat

start | Citrix Access Gatew... | Adobe Photoshop - ... | Classroom Suite - [gi... | 1:15 PM Sunday

Source: Diagram created using Classroom Suite® by Intellitools, Inc. Used with the permission of Intellitools, Inc.

- Copy the final gist from each student onto a PowerPoint slide. Ask each student to add a voice recording of the gist.

- Post the final gist to a class blog that is regularly updated. Mrs. Williams developed a free blog at *Blogger,* a service provided by Google (www.blogger.com). For purposes of Internet safety, she was careful that the blog was developed as a private site accessible only to her students and other individuals she selected.

- Structure an electronic read-around, a classroom activity adapted from an idea described by Monroe (2007) to extend the literacy conversation. This activity generally takes place in a computer lab, but can occur in any environment with one-to-one computing. Each student opens the file, and sets the cap lock on or changes the font type setting. Students then rotate to a different computer and read the selection on the screen, making comments directly on the writing and initialing their work (the new writing is obvious due to the change in font). The file with comments is saved to a new file, and the students decide whether to revise using the new material.

Extending New Learning

Strategy: RAFT Writing

Technology Applications

Digital story projects are developed using commonly available word processors and visual editors. Sufficient computers for individaul or group access are needed, as well as a specialized multimedia program, Intellipics Studio, for students needing extra literacy support.

Software Used in This Example: Microsoft Word, Intellipics Studio, Movie Maker

Recall that when using the RAFT strategy, students are able to extend their learning by taking a unique point of view different from their own and writing from that perspective. This point of view may be selected by the student, guided by the teacher, or assigned.

Smith and Throne (2007) suggest using a graphic organizer to introduce the RAFT strategy and the possible combinations of points of view that it offers (see Figure 5.9). In this example, Mrs. Williams developed a graphic organizer using a simple table in a word processor, but it could also be developed using concept mapping software, such as Inspiration.

In the first example, the format of a letter and the audience, "To Myself" was chosen by one of Mrs. Williams's students. The

FIGURE 5.9

Graphic Organizer for the RAFT Strategy

Role	Audience	Form	Topic
Heroine of today	Myself	Diary entry	A heroic deed
Newscaster	Class	Digital story	Newsflash—Girl finds little boy and becomes a heroine!
Me	Friend	Telephone conversation	You would not believe what happened! I found this little boy lost in the parking lot . . .
Friend	Another friend	Telephone conversation	What happened to Tory today at the store? Watch the 6 o'clock news!

letter to her diary follows. This letter was composed using basic word-processing skills.

Dear Diary,

Today someone called me a "little heroine." I don't think of myself as one, but I felt good hearing it. I guess I was a heroine if you think doing a normal, everyday good deed is heroic. Here's what happened. My mother and I were at the store. Mom asked me to go back to the car to get something. As I walked to the car, I saw a little boy wandering around in the parking lot. He was only about three and he looked lost. He was wandering around right in front of cars. I grabbed his hand and walked him to our car. I was hoping I would see his mother or father looking for him, but I didn't see anyone like that. I kept asking him where his parents were, but he was too little to tell me. I decided to take him into the store and ask mom what to do. When I found mom, she was surprised to see me with the little boy. Did I tell

you he said his name was Tim? Anyway, just about that time,
a voice came over the store speaker asking if anyone had
found a little boy wandering alone in the store. Mom and I
brought Tim to the manager and there his mother was. She
was crying because she thought Tim had been kidnapped.
She hugged him and hugged me for finding him. That's
when she called me her little heroine. Pretty cool, eh?

Bye for now,
Tory

For students who are younger or need additional support,
you may consider structuring the task with the use of a template. Figure 5.10 shows a letter-writing template Mrs. Williams
developed for her struggling learners using Intellipics Studio,
a program in the integrated software package Classroom Suite.
Note the features shown in this template. There are directions
to the students, which may be read aloud by clicking on one of
the "talking" bubbles at the top left corner. The buttons labeled
"Yesterday," "Today," and "Tomorrow" reveal hidden toolbars
with sentence starter phrases (such as "I found" or "I went").
The phrase is automatically copied to the document when the
button is clicked. As students enter the text of their letter, they
are assisted by "word prediction" selections based on the first
letter typed and on sentence grammar. These word prediction selections are found at the bottom of the screen. A click on
any of these words enters that word into the document. Mrs.
Williams's students personalized the stationery by a choice
of stationery styles listed on the left of the screen, and a voice
note explains how the date should be written. The text can
be read as it is typed, and the spell check feature "speaks" all
word choices. The example shown is the original template. The
instructions could easily be modified to explain the RAFT writing strategy.

FIGURE 5.10

RAFT Strategy Using a Template from Intellipics Studio®

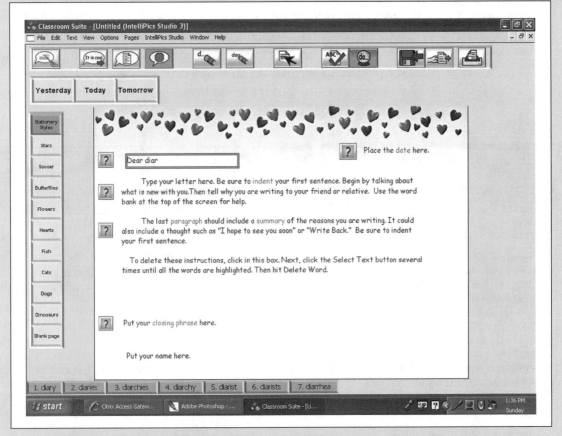

Source: Diagram created using Classroom Suite® by Intellitools, Inc. Used with the permission of Intellitools, Inc.

As the graphic organizer (Figure 5.9) indicates, Mrs. Williams knew the RAFT strategy was not limited to a letter-writing format, so she harnessed the power of the technology to motivate her students in ways that paper and pencil could not. For example, Tory and the other struggling learners were given the option to tell her story by creating a digital story using still images, music, and a narrative.

Kajder, Bull, and Albaugh (2005) offer a practical guide for developing digital stories in classrooms when time and equipment are limited. Mindful of these steps, Mrs. Williams created alternative ways for her students to construct their RAFTs. They are outlined here using Tory's heroine example.

1. Students wrote an initial script that was short and contained only the essential elements of the story to serve as a guide for what to say—the exact words do not need to be written out. This script may be written on an index card or composed using a word processor—but it should be no longer than one page. See Figure 5.11 for Tory's script.

FIGURE 5.11

Using Alternative RAFT Formats: A Script for a Digital Story

Announcer Joel: In breaking news, Tory Jones became a little heroine at Walmart today.

Tory, a 4th-grader at Skyview Elementary School, was shopping when she noticed Tim Rodriquez, a 3-year-old boy who was wandering outside from car to car in the excessive heat, crying and calling for his mother. Channel 10 correspondent Katie Smith has an exclusive interview with our latest heroine, Tory Jones.

Katie Smith: Tory, how did this rescue happen?

Tory: I was at Walmart with my mother . . . went back to the car to get her purse . . . saw Tim crying and wandering out in front of cars . . . I talked nice to him, took him by the hand, and told him we would find his mother.

Katie Smith: Then what happened?

Tory: I took him to my mother . . . an announcement came on asking that if anyone saw a lost 3-year-old answering to the name of Tim to please notify the manager . . . My Mom and I took him to the front of the store . . . The manager and Tim's mother were there.

Katie Smith: So what did Tim's Mom do?

Tory: Cried, hugged him, hugged me, called me a heroine.

Katie Smith: So do you feel like a heroine?

Tory: No—I was just doing an everyday thing, just trying to help.

Katie Smith: That's it folks, the latest in our series on everyday heroes. This is Katie Smith, Action 10 news. Back to you, Joel.

Figure 5.12

Using Alternative RAFT Formats: A Digital Story Storyboard

Storyboard

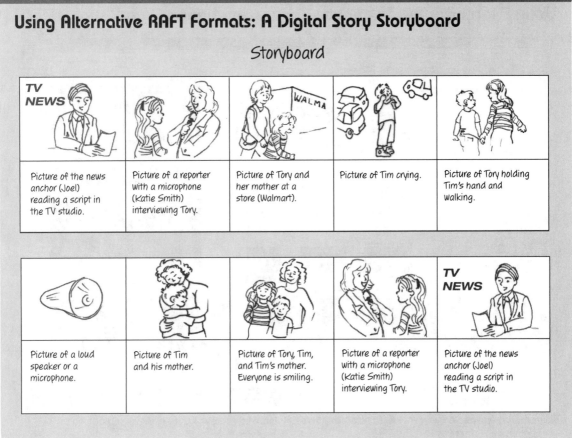

2. The second step was for the students to develop a storyboard, a series of sketched pictures, that depicted what to show (see Figure 5.12). This storyboard was developed away from the computer as an organizational strategy and to maximize the time that was spent with access to the machines. About 10 to 12 images are enough to depict a two-minute digital story. Once the storyboard was completed, students gathered the digital images—from Internet sources, from personal photographs, and scanned line art.

3. The third step was to discuss and revise the script with classmates. Students retold the story and asked for input on script and image changes.

FIGURE 5.13

Using Alternative RAFT Formats: Sequencing Images in a Visual Editor

Source: Diagram created using Movie Maker® by Microsoft, Inc. Microsoft product screen shot reprinted with permission from Microsoft Corporation.

4. Next, students sequenced the images in a video editor, MovieMaker (iMovie is another editor option). This step involved importing the digital images into the project, and dragging and dropping them on the timeline. MovieMaker (and iMovie) programs are preloaded on all Windows and Macintosh computers. Online help and tutorials are readily available. Figure 5.13 depicts this step using clip art as images.

5. Students then added the narrative track. Kajder, Bull, and Albaugh (2005) recommend recording each sentence in a separate file sequenced by number. By recording the narrative, sentence by sentence, and saving it in numerical order, it was simpler for Mrs. Williams's students to revise and keep the sound file size manageable.

6. The sixth step was to add the transitions between the slides, such as a keyhole or a checkerboard, and the special effects on certain slides, such as blurring or fading. Adding these transitions and effects was fun for Mrs. Williams's students, but these transitions can distract the students from the first five steps. Keep this step as a final editing step.

7. Finally, Mrs. Williams made time for her students to add a musical sound track. Sounds were added from public domain sources, and portions of songs from commercial recordings were used. She was sure to discuss fair use in copyright law with her class so they would take care to credit the work and use only portions of it.

Looking Back

Mrs. Williams's desire to make English/language arts lessons more engaging for her students has inspired her to expand her knowledge of and skills with various technology tools. She has found that these tools are more than gimmicky add-ons to lessons, but rather are integral to learning. Because her students are eager to interact with technology, they focus on content with greater attention, process information at higher levels of meaning, think more creatively, and organize content in logical ways for further study and later recall. As you have learned in reading about Mrs. Williams's content literacy lessons, although she has developed facility with many user-friendly commercial technology programs, she has also learned how to take advantage of presentation and interactive capabilities within everyday word-processing programs. In the next chapter you will discover further ideas for technology applications in content lessons in science.

Questions for Study

- In your present capacity as a literacy coach or imagining your role as one, what could you do to bring teachers to a level of knowledge and skills about technology tools similar to that possessed by Mrs. Williams?

- With a colleague, reflect on the topics you teach and how some of the technology applications for content literacy strategies used by Mrs. Williams could be incorporated into your lessons to increase student motivation and knowledge acquisition. What specific topics, literacy strategies, and technology applications could be woven into a lesson?

- What resources are needed in your school in order to take full advantage of technology tools such as those used by Mrs. Williams? In your capacity as a literacy coach, curriculum specialist, administrator, or teacher, establish or participate in a team to explore how to acquire needed resources.

References

Bull, G., Bull, G., Blasi, L., & and Cochran, P. (1999). Electronic texts in the classroom. *Learning & Leading with Technology, 27*(4), 46–56.

Kajder, S., Bull, G., & Albaugh, S. (2005). Constructing digital stories. *Learning and Leading with Technology, 32*(5) 40–42. http://etext.lib .virginia.edu/.

Monroe, R. (2007). Electronic read-arounds. *Learning and Leading with Technology, 34*(8), 36–37.

Smith, G., & Throne, S. (2007). Differentiating by interest in elementary classrooms. *Learning and Leading with Technology, 34*(8), 34–35.

Wiggin, Kate Douglas. *Rebecca of Sunnybrook Farm*. Retrieved on May 30, 2007, from Electronic Text Center, University of Virginia Library, http://etext.lib.virginia.edu/.

Science:
Content Literacy and Technology

Seeing Forward

As you begin this new chapter reflect on what you have learned thus far about how to use technology tools to motivate students to learn, increase engagement, and expand understanding of content material. Although topics from social studies and language arts were the focus for technology integration thus far, the technology tools employed by the teachers in the classroom case studies are generalizable across content areas and can give energy to virtually any literacy strategy. What follows is another extended classroom case documenting the connections Ms. Rhee and her second-grade students made while learning about living and nonliving things.

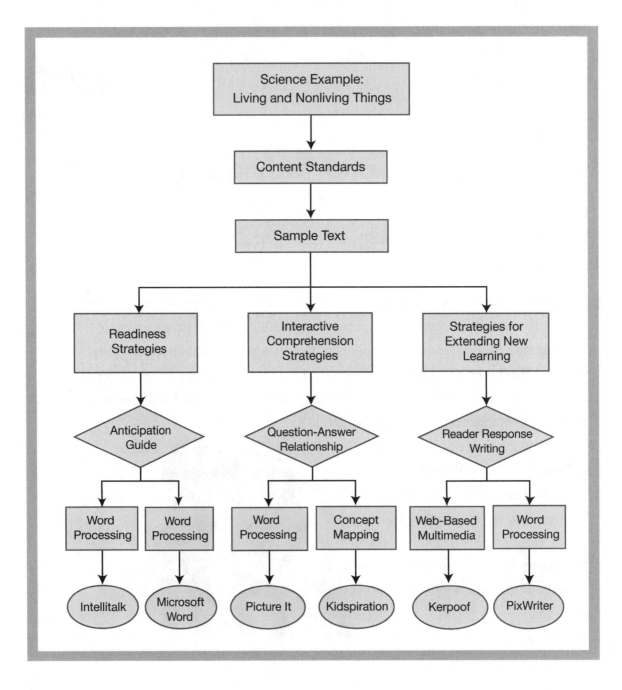

Teacher: Ms. Rhee
Grade Level: Second
Lesson Topic: Living and Nonliving Things

Content Standards

Content standards applicable to this lesson are:

- Describe inherited characteristics of living things.

- Ask questions about objects and events in the environment.

- Express data in a variety of ways by constructing illustrations, graphs, charts, tables, concept maps, and oral and written explanations as appropriate.

Sample Text for This Lesson

Living and Nonliving Things

There are many different kinds of living things on the earth. Things live in some form in the driest desert and the coldest tundra. Living things are in the deepest oceans and soaring high in the sky.

All living things need energy or food to stay alive. Some living things, like plants, can make their own food inside their cells. Humans and other animals are unable to make their own food within their cells. Animals survive by eating plants or other animals.

You might think it is easy to tell if something is living or not. Even scientists cannot give a simple definition of life. Of course, it is easy to say that a cow is living and a stone is nonliving. Even very small things that we can't see without help are living, like cells and amoebas. But with some things it is harder to tell if they are alive or not. A person, a cow, and a cell are all living because they can reproduce themselves. But so can a salt crystal. When it is put into certain mixtures of water it will grow and start to form other crystals.

It is easy to tell the difference between a cow and a stone. The difference between the simplest living thing and a nonliving thing that is not simple is harder to sort out.

Readiness

Strategy: Anticipation Guide

Technology Applications

Word processing, with text-to-speech support, classroom projection system, and computer work stations for groups of students.

Software Used in This Lesson: Intellitalk, Microsoft Word

Recall from Chapter 2 that an anticipation guide involves giving students a list of statements about the topic to be studied and asking them to respond to the statements before a full exploration of the subject. With the anticipation guide, guesses become predictions and serve as a powerful readiness to learn tool. Anticipation guides encourage students to think about what they already know and believe about a topic and help the teacher identify student misconceptions.

In this classroom description, Ms. Rhee, a second-grade teacher, prepared anticipation guide statements as an introduction to a science unit on living and nonliving things. She knew that some of her second-graders still struggled with reading and comprehension skills, so she wanted to design activities that all students would be able to be successful in completing. She also wanted to uncover an understanding of the background knowledge of her students, and any misconceptions that the students may have. She designed her anticipation guide to take advantage of the features of a text-to-speech word processor, Intellitalk. This particular word processor has ready-made templates that are easily adapted.

The example shown in Figure 6.1 from Ms. Rhee's Intellitalk lesson has buttons that are used for navigation, to read the text, and to enter the predictions "agree," "disagree," or "maybe." Other buttons "hide" or "show" the next pages of activity. Since these button actions were adapted from a preprogrammed activity suggested by the vendor, all Ms. Rhee had to do was change the button content and add the anticipation guide statements and answer blanks to the page. The students were directed to read these statements (with text-to-speech assistance if desired) and click on the appropriate

FIGURE 6.1

Anticipation Guide Using Intellitalk®, a Text-to-Speech Word Processor

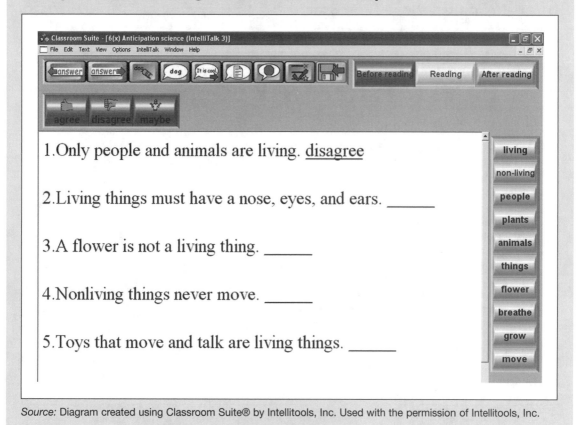

Source: Diagram created using Classroom Suite® by Intellitools, Inc. Used with the permission of Intellitools, Inc.

button for their prediction. This may be accomplished in several ways. The teacher may wish to display this page to the class, leading a discussion eliciting potential responses to the questions, or use the approach of Ms. Rhee and allow students to read and discuss the statements in small groups prior to responding. The example in Figure 6.1 shows the first question answered with "disagree."

The next step in the anticipation guide strategy is for the students to read the information and return to the guide statements to verify the correctness or incorrectness of their initial responses. Because Ms. Rhee was well aware that some of her students still struggled with reading, while others did not, she pasted a digital

FIGURE 6.2

Reading Support for the Anticipation Guide Using Intellitalk®, a Text-to-Speech Word Processor

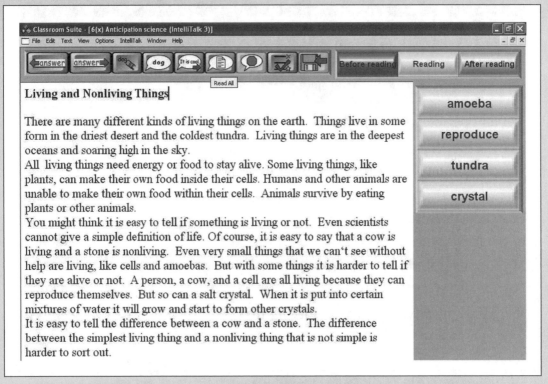

Source: Diagram created using Classroom Suite® by Intellitools, Inc. Used with the permission of Intellitools, Inc.

version of the text into the second page of this Intellitalk activity file for optional student access (see Figure 6.2). Since this passage was short, and she did not have access to a digital version, she merely typed it in. Other options, for longer text selections, are to scan the text and convert to a text file using optical character recognition software, or to obtain a digital version of the passage from the textbook publisher.

To access this page, the students clicked on the "Reading" button, which displayed the text. Here, the students could control the level of support that they needed. They may have the entire selection read to them, or, in the case of Ms. Rhee's students, only certain portions were read to them. She preplaced definitions of difficult vocabulary terms on side buttons. The students clicked on these terms to listen to a definition and its use in a sentence.

The final step, after reading and reviewing the concepts related to each statement, was for Ms. Rhee's students to look at the anticipation guide statements again and decide whether they needed to keep the same answer or change it. They also developed a short statement explaining their choices. Finding ideas and information from the text reinforced their new answer.

Figure 6.3 shows an example of this phase, in which Ms. Rhee's students revisit the statements after learning new information

FIGURE 6.3

Revisiting Anticipation Guide Statements Using Intellitalk®, a Text-to-Speech Word Processor

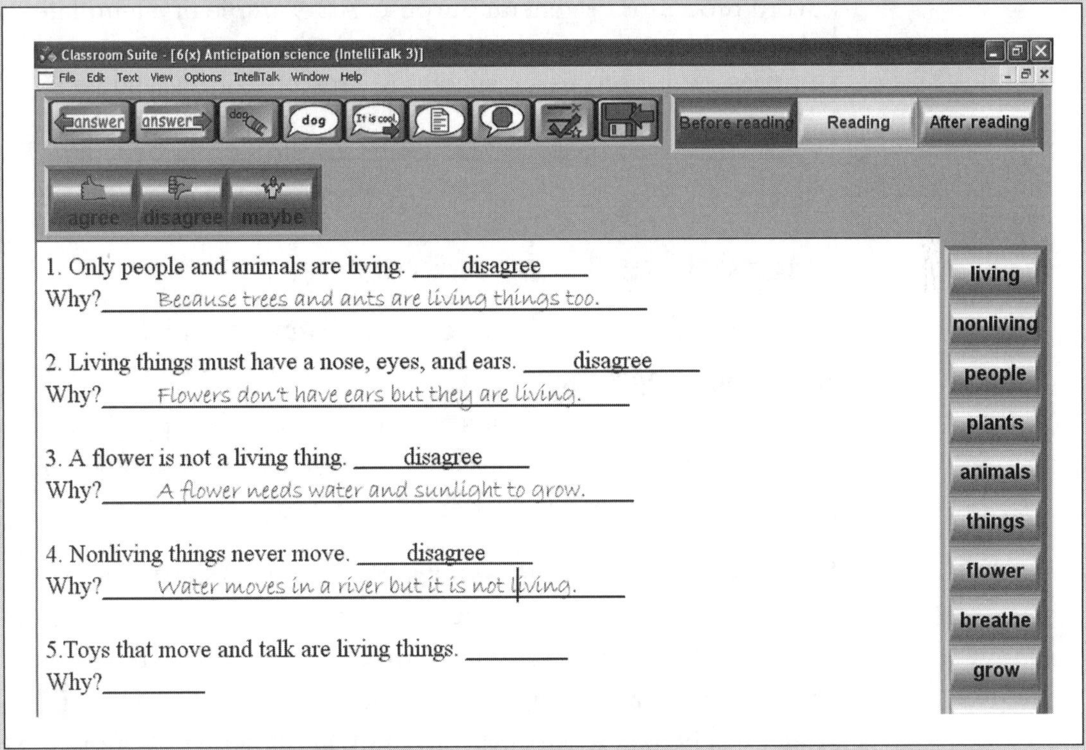

Source: Diagram created using Classroom Suite® by Intellitools, Inc. Used with the permission of Intellitools, Inc.

about living and nonliving things. Note how she developed this page. The anticipation guide statements were copied from the prereading activity. After each statement, she added the word "Why?" and inserted an answer field for the students to compose their answer. In order to support students with writing their answers, she entered several vocabulary words into the button toolbar on the right. Students clicked on the word to have it read aloud and inserted into the answer field, to be used, if desired, in composing their answers.

TIPS

In the example of an anticipation guide from Ms. Rhee's lesson, we demonstrated how a tool such as Intellitalk could be used to customize literacy supports. Don't be intimidated by the apparent complexity of this example. Anticipation guides will also work with a simple word-processing file, either text-to-speech word processor or general purpose. An example of a template developed for the anticipation guide strategy using a general purpose word processor, such as Microsoft Word, is shown in Figure 6.4.

Interactive Comprehension

Strategy: Question-Answer Relationship (QAR)

Technology Applications
Word processing, with rebus and text-to-speech support, a concept mapping program, classroom projection system, and computer work stations for groups of students.

Software Used in This Lesson: Picture It and Kidspiration
Recall from Chapter 2 that the question-answer relationship strategy, or QAR, teaches students to process information based on literal, inferential, and applied questions. The overall goal of the strategy is help students learn to think at higher levels about text,

FIGURE 6.4

Anticipation Guide Template Using a Standard Word Processor

1. Anticipation statement	Before		After	
	A	D	A	D
What did you learn?				

2. Anticipation statement	Before		After	
	A	D	A	D
What did you learn?				

3. Anticipation statement	Before		After	
	A	D	A	D
What did you learn?				

4. Anticipation statement	Before		After	
	A	D	A	D
What did you learn?				

5. Anticipation statement	Before		After	
	A	D	A	D
What did you learn?				

6. Anticipation statement	Before		After	
	A	D	A	D
What did you learn?				

7. Anticipation statement	Before		After	
	A	D	A	D
What did you learn?				

and not depend on word-for-word processing. After reading a passage, students answer related questions and determine whether the answer is "Right There" (stated word for word), "Author and Me" (requiring a combination of word-for-word and prior knowledge), or "On My Own" (requiring mostly prior knowledge). Technology can assist teachers and students in using the QAR strategy. In this example, we show how Ms. Rhee used text-to-speech and concept mapping software with this strategy.

Ms. Rhee decided to model how to use the QAR strategy with the following passage.

> Plants and animals are living things because they grow and change. Some living things move on their own. Nonliving things cannot move on their own, nor grow. A bear breathes, but a chair does not. A book cannot make copies of itself, but humans can have children. A tree makes seeds that can grow into new trees. These are some of the ways we can tell the difference between living and nonliving things.

Because some of the students in Ms. Rhee's class still struggled with word recognition, she decided to make an electronic version of the text available in Picture It, a rebus-based text-to-speech word processor. Since this was a short selection, she merely typed the text into the story text box, as shown in Figure 6.5. Then she selected "parse the text" (under the edit menu) to automatically add pictures to the words and phrases in the selection. (If the selection is too long to enter by typing, other options are to obtain digital versions of the text through scanning or through alternate electronic file formats.)

Figure 6.6 shows this same text in the reader mode view. Ms. Rhee's struggling readers practiced reading this passage and activated the text-to-speech feature as desired. They followed along as the text is highlighted and read aloud.

FIGURE 6.5

Preparing a Reading Passage Using a Rebus-Based Word Processor

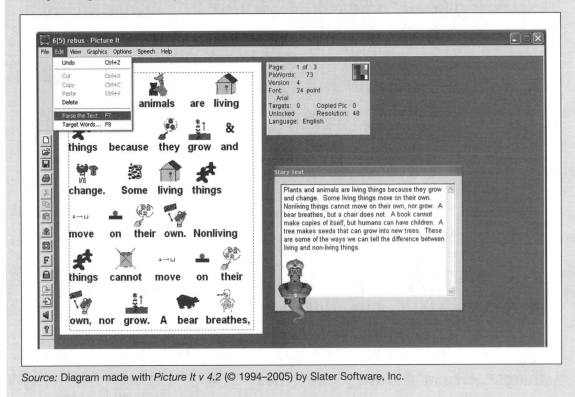

Source: Diagram made with *Picture It v 4.2* (© 1994–2005) by Slater Software, Inc.

Ms. Rhee recognized that text-to-speech is useful when developing word-recognition skills, but that her struggling readers would continue to have difficulty understanding the material without additional help (Balajthy, 2005). Comprehending the content required that her students learn the more sophisticated skills of spotting key ideas, recognizing the author's intent, and applying new information to schemas that describe what they already know. Her intent was to help her students begin to internalize higher-level thinking about the text and other sources of information. The QAR strategy assisted in developing these comprehension skills for Ms. Rhee's students. Students not only respond to questions but they

FIGURE 6.6

Reader Mode View of a Reading Passage Displayed in a Rebus-Based Word Processor

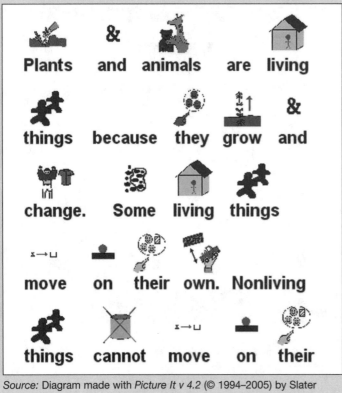

Plants and animals are living
things because they grow and
change. Some living things
move on their own. Nonliving
things cannot move on their

Source: Diagram made with *Picture It v 4.2* (© 1994–2005) by Slater Software, Inc.

also learn how to recognize how they know the answer to questions by activating their own background knowledge or calling attention to key terms. Ms. Rhee uses this strategy often, with frequent or even daily modeling and guided practice.

Ms. Rhee developed at least three questions from the content of the reading passage, each exemplifying one of the QAR question types:

1. Why are plants and animals living things?

2. Why can't a book move on its own?

3. Why is fire not a living thing, even though it can grow and it needs air?

In order to develop a visual map that will help model the strategy and direct guided practice, Ms. Rhee developed a simple Kidspiration activity and entered these questions (see Figure 6.7). She displayed this visual guide to the students, as she thought aloud, modeling her ways of thinking about the question and asking the students to help her decide the best category for each question, why, and a possible answer. She demonstrated how to move the question boxes around and reviewed how to move between picture and writing views.

Ms. Rhee then uploaded the file to student computer work stations for guided practice, and directed the children's practice. An example of one student's completed work is shown in Figure 6.8.

FIGURE 6.7

Visual Map for the QAR Strategy

Think about the answers to these questions. Move each question to the super grouper that describes its type. Then switch to writing view and answer the question.

1 Why are plants and animals living things?

2 Why can't a book move on its own?

3 Why is fire not a living thing, even though it can grow and it needs air?

Right There

Author and Me

On My Own

Source: Diagram created in Kidspiration® by Inspiration Software®, Inc.

FIGURE 6.8

Student Response Using a Visual Map for the QAR Strategy

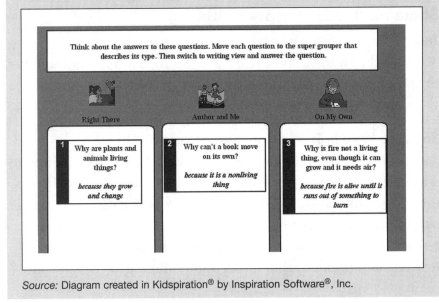

Think about the answers to these questions. Move each question to the super grouper that describes its type. Then switch to writing view and answer the question.

Right There

Author and Me

On My Own

1 Why are plants and animals living things?

because they grow and change

2 Why can't a book move on its own?

because it is a nonliving thing

3 Why is fire not a living thing, even though it can grow and it needs air?

because fire is alive until it runs out of something to burn

Source: Diagram created in Kidspiration® by Inspiration Software®, Inc.

TIPS

The QAR strategy is a versatile strategy that is easily adapted to a variety of other technology applications. Consider the following:

- The QAR strategy is meant to develop critical comprehension skills. The strategy assumes that the text in question could be easily read by the students. The reality of most classrooms, however, is that many students still need word recognition support. Appropriate word recognition skills are necessary, but not sufficient, skills for the development of critical comprehension abilities.

- We showed how a rebus-based word processor could be used to support word recognition skills for primary students. For older students still needing word recognition support, consider scanning a short passage, converting it to digital text (suggested programs include Kurzweil 3000, Read and Write Gold, or any of the OCR programs that come with a scanner). Open the file in a text-to-speech program (as previously described, or use shareware such as ReadPlease), and type the QAR questions directly on to pertinent sections of the text.

- QAR activities, with room to insert questions and answers, could also be developed using a simple word processor. Consider setting up the initial format without content, and save it as a template.

Extending New Learning

Strategy: Reader Response Writing

Technology Applications

Multimedia presentations, word processing, with rebus and text-to-speech support, classroom projection system, and computer work stations for groups of students

Software Used in This Lesson: Kerpoof and PixWriter

As the science unit on living and nonliving things was coming to a close, Ms. Rhee felt generally satisfied with the students' progress. She planned and delivered a mixture of hands-on activities as well as content area learning strategies. Combining technology with content literacy, she engaged students in reading and learning about the topic of living and nonliving, as well as introduced them to a variety of ways to practice critical thinking and analysis skills in science. To conclude the unit, Ms. Rhee decided to give her students the opportunity to find personal links to the newly learned content by prompting reader response writing.

In Chapter 2 we described how the reader response strategy makes it possible for students to explore personal connections to information and concepts in the content areas. This strategy takes students through a question-and-answering process intended to reveal students' feelings and attitudes related to what has been learned and then to invoke experiences in support of those feelings and attitudes.

Ms. Rhee decided to use a multimedia program to assist the students in composing their reader responses. There are several reasons behind her selection of a multimedia program with this strategy. Multimedia programs allow students flexibility in expression, making it easier for them to pair personal expression and connections with literacy skills. They can illustrate their thoughts with pictures, artwork, text, and sound. Multimedia programs are valuable resources when getting students to work together, hence they foster collaboration skills. Scientists use a variety of multimedia programs in communicating their work, and introducing young students to communication using multimedia representations can help them begin to think like scientists. Ms. Rhee selected Kerpoof (www.kerpoof.com), a free program that is easy for the students to use. Kerpoof is a Web-based program, making it readily available for use from school or home. Since the program, as well as the students' work, can be accessed from anywhere, the work is not bound by the confines of a particular computer or machine. Kerpoof is also designed so that the student can share the work with selected others who can also access it online, thus providing a platform for developing beginning collaboration skills in science.

In setting up the assignment, Ms. Rhee asked the students to respond with words and pictures to the following three questions.

- What was the most interesting thing you learned?

- Why is this so interesting to you?

- What can you say about yourself to explain why you think this is so interesting?

Kerpoof "pages" are easy and fun to illustrate, but in order to have enough room for pictures and text, she used the "story" feature. The students answered each question on a different page, resulting in three pictures each.

Ms. Rhee knew that one student in particular, Devon, would need help with this assignment. She asked him to answer the questions with pictures and drawings, then to tell her the answers. Here is what Devon said:

> I like learning about the plants that eat flies. I think it would be cool to have a plant like that. I would feed it bugs. I like stuff like that. I like to look at this funny book in the library. It has pictures of all kinds of things. I bet it will have a picture of a plant that catches bugs.

Working with a partner, Devon found an interesting background, decorated it with related pictures, and typed his script into Kerpoof. Figure 6.9 shows what his final product looked like.

Ms. Rhee wanted to reinforce further Devon's writing skills. She was able to give him extra, differentiated practice by using PixWriter, a rebus-based talking word processor that is a companion program to Picture It (Slater Software).

Ms. Rhee typed Devon's words into the typing area of the PixWriter, as shown in Figure 6.10. The program automatically sprayed the buttons in the grid area at the bottom of the screen with each word. A bit of manipulation of the order—moving nouns, verbs, and pronouns near each other—and Devon had an individualized practice activity. He could write his sentences by

FIGURE 6.9

Example of Reader-Response Writing

Source: Diagram created using Kerpoof by Kerpoof.com

FIGURE 6.10

Support for the Reader-Response Writing Strategy

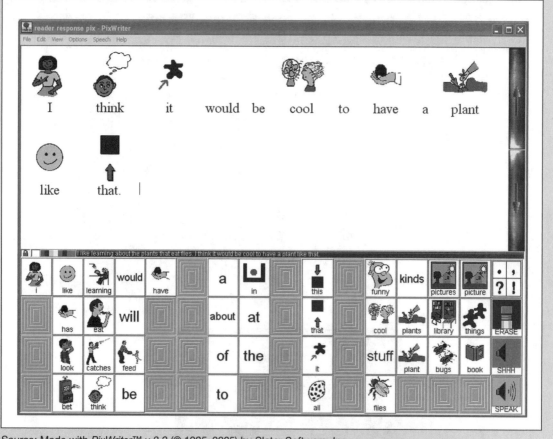

Source: Made with *PixWriter™ v 2.2* (© 1995–2005) by Slater Software, Inc.

clicking on each word to display it in the typed area. He learned to copy and paste his sentences into other applications, such as another Kerpoof story. As Devon became more fluent, Ms. Rhee chose to eliminate some of the button choices, and eventually hid the grid completely.

TIPS

- Multimedia representations are appropriate for all age and grade levels. Other multimedia programs suitable for use in schools include Hyperstudio and PowerPoint. Intellipics Studio, a companion program to Intellitalk within the Classroom Suite programs, has an extensive picture library, a drawing program, text-to-speech, and templates that could be adapted for use with these strategies.

- Multimedia tools seem to be most effective when students use them together, manipulating representations and discussing their findings. When they engage in these types of activities, they are developing the same kind of skills that scientists use to reason and argue theories effectively. (CITED, 2007)

- Remember Internet safety procedures; bookmark sites with digital pictures for younger students or use programs with picture libraries and drawing programs.

- Encourage students to use digital cameras to capture ideas for their presentations.

- Adapt reader response questions for science lessons to include prompts that encourage the development of expert scientific language, specific phrases, and language that scientists use to communicate with their peers. Tan, Yeo, and Lim (2005) suggest the following sentence starters:

I hypothesize that . . .

I observed that . . .

My research shows that . . .

My theory doesn't explain why . . .

A better theory might be . . .

Looking Back

As Ms. Rhee demonstrated, science topics can be interesting and accessible when structured around lessons that pair content literacy strategies with technology tools. Particularly noteworthy is how Ms. Rhee took advantage of software that offers students multimedia presentations of information and strategies in order to make learning active and interactive for competent and less competent readers and writers. In addition, the TIPS sections helped you envision how simple, ever-present software programs can be used in the service of content learning and content literacy. Finally, as with all the literacy strategies and technology tools described in the content area case study chapters, those employed by Ms. Rhee can be woven into units of study to help students meet virtually any content standard.

Questions for Study

- With a colleague, reflect on the content delivery adaptations Ms. Rhee made for her struggling readers and learners and consider the kinds of adaptations the two of you would need to make to respond to the needs of your less able readers. What technology tools could help both of you deliver content and strategies to struggling readers that would engender active and interactive learning?

- Based on the TIPS sections in this chapter, explore the formatting and interactive capabilities of the word-processing programs already loaded on your personal and classroom computer(s). Using an anticipation guide, QAR, or reader-response writing strategy, apply the available technology tools from the word-processing program to make the strategy interactive.

■ In your role as a literacy coach, classroom teacher, or administrator, how can you acquire and develop the multimedia skills described in this chapter to facilitate children's and/or colleagues' skill development? With a group, discuss and plan professional development opportunities around gaining competence with these software tools.

References

Balajthy, E. (2005, January/February). Text-to-speech software for helping struggling readers. *Reading Online, 8*(4).
Available at www.readingonline.org/articles/art_index
.asp?HREF=balajthy2/index.html.

Center for Implementing Technology in Education. (2007). *Using multimedia tools to help students learn science.* Accessed on June 21, 2007, from www.cited.org/index.aspx?page_id=148.

Tan, S. C., Yeo, A. C. J., & Lim, W. Y. (2005). Changing epistemology of science learning through inquiry with computer-supported collaborative learning. *Journal of Computers in Mathematics and Science Teaching, 24*(4), 367–386.

CHAPTER 7

Math:
Content Literacy and Technology

Seeing Forward

In this final content area chapter, you will discover various ways Mr. Cooper employed technology tools to format content literacy strategies to help his students learn about geometry. As you read, notice how Mr. Cooper took full advantage of the Internet and available software options in most Word programs to present the strategies in simple ways that encouraged active student

participation. You should also note how these literacy strategies and technology tools have the potential to be applied to teaching and learning topics from a range of content areas.

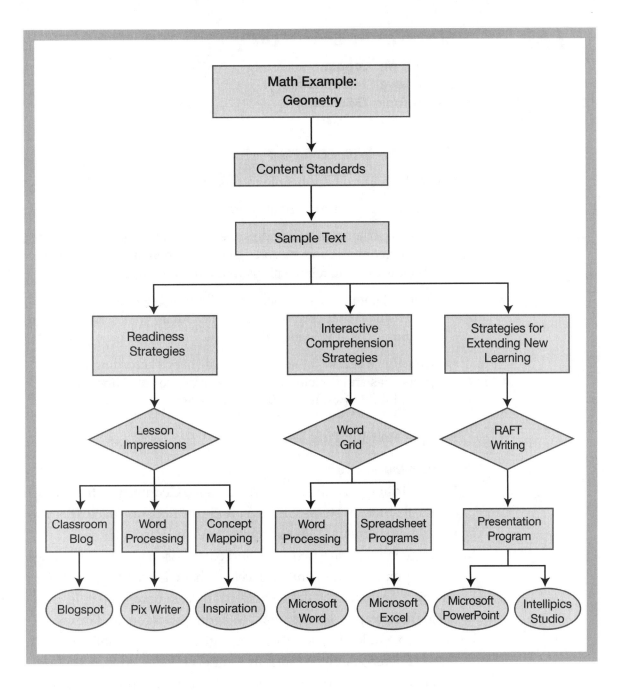

Classroom Case Study

Teacher: Mr. Cooper
Grade Level: Intermediate
Lesson Topic: Geometry

Content Standards

Content standards applicable to this lesson are:

- Identify and use appropriate terminology for geometrical elements.

- Analyze characteristics and properties of two- and three-dimensional geometric shapes and develop mathematical arguments about geometric relationships (NCTM Standard).

- Identify, compare, and analyze attributes of two- and three-dimensional shapes and develop vocabulary to describe the attributes (NCTM Standard).

- Classify two- and three-dimensional shapes according to their properties and develop definitions of classes of shapes such as triangles and pyramids (NCTM Standard).

Sample Text for This Lesson

What Is Geometry?

Circles, triangles, and squares are shapes. Geometry is the mathematical study of shapes, figures, and positions in space. It is useful in many careers such as architecture and carpentry.

In geometry, measurements and comparisons are made of lines, angles, points, planes, and surfaces. A shape is the outer form of an object or figure such as a circle, triangle, square, rectangle, parallelogram, trapezoid, rhombus, octagon, pentagon, and hexagon. There are equilateral, isosceles, and right triangles. A solid is a three-dimensional figure such as a cube, cylinder, cone, prism, or pyramid. Other solid shapes include the tetrahedron and octahedron. Positions in space are things like points, lines, and angles.

Formulas can be used to figure out the dimensions of shapes and figures. Instruments such as rulers, triangles, compasses, and protractors are used in geometry. Today, many people also use graphing calculators and computers in geometry.

The Greeks made many contributions to our understanding of geometry. For example, Archimedes is credited as the first to calculate the ratio between a circle's diameter and its circumference, now known as pi. Pythagoras is famous for his theorem, which states that in any right-angled triangle the sum of the squares on the two shorter sides equals the square of the hypotenuse. However, many people think the Egyptians and Babylonians knew this math much earlier.

Readiness

Strategy: Lesson Impression

Technology Applications

Classroom blog, with optional support from concept mapping, standard word processing, and rebus-based word processing.

Software Used in This Lesson

Any of a number of free, classroom blog programs, with optional use of Inspiration, Microsoft Word, and PixWriter.

Recall from Chapter 2 that the lesson impression strategy exposes students to the content to be read by giving them just enough information in the form of key terms and phrases to activate their prior knowledge and develop an "impression," which serves as a prediction to be compared with the actual content. This strategy also gives the teacher valuable impressions regarding the students' understandings of those terms. Presented with the important vocabulary and phrases extracted from the text to be read, students develop an impression in the form of a narrative or a description of what they will be learning, using these words. Students then share their impression with other members of the class.

A classroom blog is a technology application that is especially suited to this strategy, as Mr. Cooper, the fifth-grade math teacher discovered. A blog is simply a website (a we_b_-based _log_, hence the term _blog_) where anyone may post information on a particular topic. Once posted, the information can be read and responded to by others. Some blogs are open for posting, viewing, and commenting by the general public; others are developed as private sites with a defined membership and posting controls.

A number of websites offer a system for developing free, safe, and easy-to-use, teacher-controlled classroom blogs (see resources at the end of this chapter for a listing). Teachers initiate a classroom blog through a verification process. Once the classroom blog is registered and the students are signed up, the teacher sets up a posting, or assignment. Students compose a short article related to the assignment, and post it to the blog. In most educational blog sites, there is a system for reviewing postings and comments—the teacher approves the posting, or asks the student to revise it. Once the posting is approved, it is published, and classmates and other audiences read and reply to the article. The teacher also controls the replies, approving comments prior to posting. Thus, the security and social networking features support the literacy process of the classroom blog—submit, revise, approve; comment, revise, approve.

In the example shown in Figure 7.1, Mr. Cooper took words describing geometrical shapes taken from the sample reading selection. He posted these words to a classroom blog, along with directions. An example of his directions, a student response from José, and a comment from Mary are shown.

Even though blogging supports a causal style of writing, Mr. Cooper knew that developing an acceptable posting would not be an automatic process for all his students. His more fluent writers were easily able to compose their post on the blog input screen, but his struggling learners benefited from the literacy support that a word processor or concept mapping software provided. Here are some suggestions, based on Mr. Cooper's experiences, for using alternative technology tools with which to apply lesson impressions.

Example of Using Blogs with the Lesson Impressions Strategy

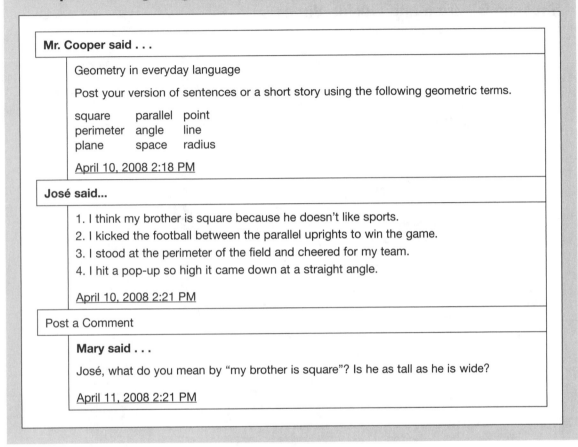

Mr. Cooper said . . .

Geometry in everyday language

Post your version of sentences or a short story using the following geometric terms.

square	parallel	point
perimeter	angle	line
plane	space	radius

<u>April 10, 2008 2:18 PM</u>

José said...

1. I think my brother is square because he doesn't like sports.
2. I kicked the football between the parallel uprights to win the game.
3. I stood at the perimeter of the field and cheered for my team.
4. I hit a pop-up so high it came down at a straight angle.

<u>April 10, 2008 2:21 PM</u>

Post a Comment

Mary said . . .

José, what do you mean by "my brother is square"? Is he as tall as he is wide?

<u>April 11, 2008 2:21 PM</u>

In using the lesson impression strategy, students use their initial impressions to guide the learning process. As they read, they are directed to pay attention to what they are learning, notice how it compares to their initial impressions, and keep a record of similarities and differences between their initial impressions and the actual text. Mr. Cooper used the program Inspiration as a technology tool in this process. Figure 7.2 is an example of Mr. Cooper's display of the nine "lesson impression" words in a concept mapping format. This map was created during a discussion with the students, using the "rapid fire" tools to form quick and

FIGURE 7.2

Concept Map of Lesson Impression Strategy, Showing Diagram and Outline Views

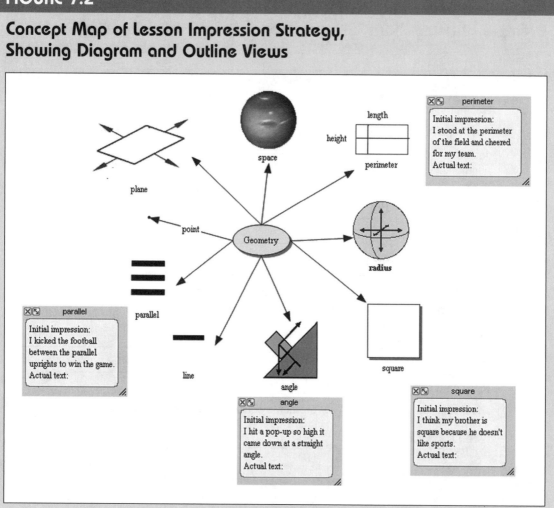

Source: Diagram created in Inspiration® by Inspiration Software®, Inc.

easy links from the main idea to the impression words. During the interactive discussion, the students were able to recommend pictures for the concepts using the picture library and other clip art sources. Mr. Cooper added a blank note to each concept, and directed his students to write their impressions, sentences, or ideas in this note section. The file was saved as a template, and then synched to his students who had hand-helds and to those

FIGURE 7.2 (continued)

Geometry		
I. square	**IV. line**	**VII. radius**
Initial impression I think my brother is square because he doesn't like sports. Actual text	Initial impression Actual text	Initial impression Actual text
II. parallel	**V. plane**	**VIII. point**
Initial impression I kicked the football between the parallel uprights to win the game. Actual text	Initial impression Actual text	Initial impression Actual text
III. angle	**VI. space**	**IX. perimeter**
Initial impression I hit a pop up so high it came down at a straight angle. Actual text	Initial impression Actual text	Initial impression I stood at the perimeter of the field and cheered for my team. Actual text

with laptop computers. (Obviously, there are other ways to transfer this type of file to student computer work stations besides synchronization for classes that do not have this equipment—uploading to a class or school server, emailing, or copying to a disc or flash drive. And for classrooms that operate with only one computer station, the picture and outline views of the file may be printed for student use as worksheets.) Once the template was transferred, Mr. Cooper gave his students the option of composing their thoughts in diagram or the outline view of the program, or of transferring it to a word processor for further input.

In this example, note that José entered impressions for *perimeter*, *parallel*, *angle*, and *square* into the note section, hiding and showing the notes as desired. Once he was satisfied with his work, he copied and pasted his sentences to his post on the classroom blog. When José began to read the text on geometric terms, he would have the option of switching to the outline view to take notes, comparing his sentences to what the actual text said about each concept. José could choose to compose these thoughts within the Inspiration program itself (it comes equipped with a spell check and word guide feature) or transfer his work to a word processor (such as Microsoft Word) for further editing.

For younger students, English language learners, or other students who could benefit from scaffolded literacy support, consider using a specialized word processor. PixWriter is an example of rebus-word processor—one that automatically associates a picture with a word. PixWriter has a library of 6,000 pictures, which are used to reference over 10,000 words. The words are read aloud as they are typed, and students can write in either English or Spanish. One particularly useful feature is the easy-to-use writing set-up, in which students can write by selecting buttons filled with pictures and words. In addition to the extensive picture library, the program has the option of incorporating additional or alternate pictures and clip art for standard picture-vocabulary associations. Figure 7.3 is an example of José's first sentence impression using *PixWriter* with a writing set-up. Once his story is completed, José can copy the text and paste it into his blog posting.

Interactive Comprehension

Strategy: Word Grid

Technology Applications

Word processor and personal computers (laptops or hand-helds)

Software Used in This Lesson: Microsoft Word

Other Possibilities: Spreadsheet programs (as found in Appleworks, Microsoft Works, or Microsoft Excel) Inspire Data, Read and Write Gold (texthelp)

FIGURE 7.3

**Example of Lesson Impression Strategy
Using PixWriter® by Slater Software, Inc.**

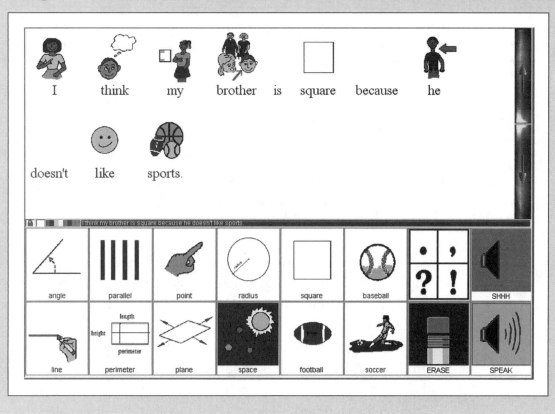

Word grids are often used to teach and to learn critical vocabulary in an organized visual manner. Using a word grid, students record the essential features, concepts, or ideas of key terms in a chart format. When using this strategy, the teacher either assigns key terms to the grid for students to complete, or the students gather related vocabulary words and key features to help build the grid. Using a legend that connects the content term with the feature, students fill in the grid as they progress through an exploration of the topic.

FIGURE 7.4

Example of a Word Grid Using the Tables Feature of a Standard Word Processor

Geometric Terms	4-Sided	Sides of Equal Length	Sides Are Parallel	Others: (list)
parallelogram	yes	no	yes	
polygon				
rectangle	yes	no	yes	
square	yes	yes	yes	

Legend:
yes = feature is present, no = feature is not present, maybe = feature is sometimes present.

Pairing technology with word grids offers the opportunity for students to develop comprehension skills while using technology in the context of a genuine task. Word grids may be developed in several ways.

Mr. Cooper guided his students in developing a word grid from a standard word processor (see Figure 7.4). He demonstrated how to build a 5×5 table, 5 columns and 5 rows, from the table icon on the standard Microsoft Word toolbar. He designated the first row (horizontal axis) as a title row, and labeled the first cell in the first row "Geometric Terms." Together, the class skimmed the text to determine the terms that were being studied, then listed them in the first column (the vertical axis). Next, as they read the textbook and engaged in class discussion, they determined important features of each of these terms, and listed them across the column headings. Finally, they developed a legend: "yes" indicated the feature was present, "no" meant the feature was not present, and "maybe" indicated the feature could sometimes be present. Mr. Cooper then showed his class how to add more columns and more rows to the table in case they were needed for new terms or as yet undescribed features (using table>insert>row or column).

As the students read the selection, they filled in pertinent features of terms listed in the word grid and added new features and new terms as needed. Once the grid was complete, the teacher led a discussion intended to help the students discover the shared and the unique characteristics of the key terms. The example in Figure 7.4 is quite simple. It contains few terms and few features; similarities and differences can easily be discerned visually (e.g., Which of these geometric figures has 4 sides? Which figures do not have 4 sides?). However, many text-based readings have a much greater number of terms and features that need to be analyzed in order to be better understood. In these cases, technology can add efficiency to the process of learning and analyzing the vocabulary terms.

For example, in most word processors, the tables have a sort feature that enables the table content to be sorted by at least three variables. Therefore, the teacher may ask or students may ask of each other or themselves the question, Which figures have parallel sides that are not of equal length?

By activating the sort feature (see screen shot, Figure 7.5), the table order changes. According to this new visual display, the parallelogram and the rectangle are sorted together, each having those characteristics (see Figure 7.6).

FIGURE 7.5

The Dialog Box for the Sort Feature in MS Word 2003®

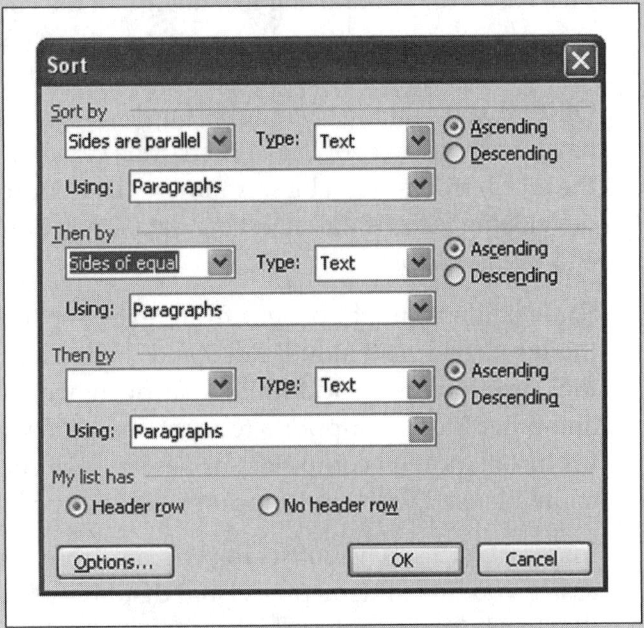

Source: Microsoft product screen shot reprinted with permission from Microsoft Corporation.

FIGURE 7.6

Example of a Sorted Word Grid

Geometric Terms	4-Sided	Sides of Equal Length	Sides Are Parallel	Others: (list)
polygon				
parallelogram	yes	no	yes	
rectangle	yes	no	yes	
square	yes	yes	yes	

Legend:
yes = feature is present, no = feature is not present, maybe = feature is sometimes present.

TIPS

Consider these other software options:

- This basic concept of using technology in the context of a genuine task—in this case developing word grids—could be extended to other software programs. Spreadsheets, such as those offered in Appleworks, Microsoft Works, and Microsoft Office (Excel), are excellent tools for developing charts and graphs. Spreadsheets have much greater sorting and analysis capabilities than the simple options shown in the word-processing tables. A number of resources are available to assist teachers in developing lessons for analyzing data. They are listed in the resources section at the end of this chapter.

- Some students might benefit from text-to-speech features, or having the content of the word grid read aloud. Read and Write Gold (Texthelp) is a software package that functions as an add-on toolbar designed to provide text-to-speech capabilities and other literacy supports to most computer programs. It is currently available for installation on computers or network servers, or as a portable USB device that could be used with any computer without program installation.

- InspireData is a new software program from Inspiration, Inc. that is designed to assist students in depicting visual displays of data. This program may be useful in the development and analysis of the content of large word grids.

- Finally, for teachers who are still struggling with the one-computer classroom, using a word processor to construct word grids is still possible. Although it will not be possible for students to use the interactive features of the word processor without access to individual stations, the teacher may still use word processing or spreadsheets to construct the grids and print them on paper for the students to complete.

Extending New Learning

Strategy: RAFT Writing

Technology Applications

Digital storytelling using presentation programs, student access to computers for individual use or use by teams

Software Used in This Lesson: Microsoft PowerPoint
Other Possibilities: HyperStudio, Intellipics Studio

Writing in math is a powerful tool. It offers students the opportunity to articulate their thoughts for themselves and others and provides teachers with insights into students' knowledge and understanding (Sibley, 2003). By writing in math, students learn to express mathematical ideas in ways that make sense to them and further develop their ability to communicate mathematical concepts through more conventional representations. Standards from the National Council for Teachers of Mathematics (NCTM) support nurturing the ability to write about mathematics across the grades. Furthermore, math standards in communication state that:

Instructional programs from pre-kindergarten through grade 12 should enable all students to—
- organize and consolidate their mathematical thinking through communication;
- communicate their mathematical thinking coherently and clearly to peers, teachers, and others;
- analyze and evaluate the mathematical thinking and strategies of others;
- use the language of mathematics to express mathematical ideas precisely. (NCTM, 2000)

The RAFT writing strategy is well suited to encourage these abilities. Recall that students use the letters of the RAFT acronym (R—role of writer; A—audience; F—format; T—topic) to write a short topic-focused piece based on newly learned information, processes, and concepts. The designations for each letter of RAFT can either be given to the students or the students can be allowed the freedom to choose their own role, audience, and format when composing a RAFT. In this example, Mr. Cooper paired the RAFT strategy with digital storytelling procedures. He used the following steps when incorporating RAFT. (These steps were modified from advice on using digital books to teach math, developed by Wilkerson, 2001.)

1. The first step was to identify the mathematical concept(s) to be addressed. In this case, the concept was the occurrence of geometric shapes in everyday life.

2. Mr. Cooper determined that his students would create the digital stories as an extension of their learning about geometric shapes. (Other uses for digital stories include introductory, developmental, and review lessons.)

3. He identified the RAFT strategy to guide the character(s) and story line, and worked with the students to create individual RAFT outlines.

4. He then asked the students to create a storyboard—developing the script and sketches of the pictures they would use in each slide. He limited their assignment to between 5 and 10 slides.

5. Mr. Cooper gave the students a choice of presentation format (e.g., HyperStudio or PowerPoint) and set up a template for the project—title page and 5 slides with forward and back navigation buttons. He organized the digital cameras for check-out and made the classroom scanner available. After the students had developed a storyboard sketching out the contents of each slide, he directed them to gather pictures using the camera, scanners, clip art, and drawing software.

6. Using the presentation software, the students put their book together, using text, pictures, and recording their own narrations.

Some students worked with a partner, others worked independently, depending on their skills and the nature of their project.

7. When the digital story was completed, he instructed the students to save it in a Read-Only format (so that it could not be altered), and to make a backup of their work.

James and Tory created the following RAFT outline:

Role: *square*
Audience: *a circle*
Format: *a cell phone conversation; told in multimedia format*
Topic: *What I Did Saturday Night*

Next, James and Tory developed the following script for their storyboard. The script is a rough draft of the text that they will show and what they will narrate in the slides. It may be modified as the slides develop.

Rrrinnnnngggggggg!

Circle: Hello.

Square: Hi, it's me.

Circle: Oh hi. How are you?

Square: Great. Listen, I have to tell you what I did Saturday night.

Circle: I'm sure you had more fun than me.

Square: I'll bet I did, too. I was walking around town and it seemed everywhere I looked I was being honored. First I went to the art museum and there I was in the picture frame of many famous paintings. Then I took a walk down Main Street and I was there on signs and boxes and even little kids' building blocks in the window of the toy store.

Circle: Wow, you really are popular.

Square: Yeah, well, when you can be found just about everywhere you look, you'd be popular, too.

From the draft script, the students drew out a storyboard and then gathered pictures to illustrate their digital story. The pictures may be taken with a digital camera, hand drawn and scanned into a computer file, clip art, or Internet pictures. James and Tory

FIGURE 7.7

Example of Using a Digital Story with the RAFT Writing Strategy

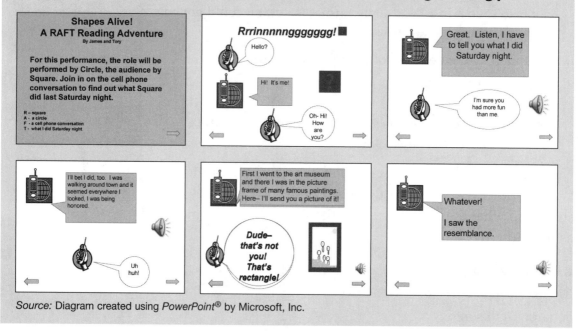

Source: Diagram created using *PowerPoint*® by Microsoft, Inc.

then put the script, pictures, and narration together in the template developed by the teacher. The example shown in Figure 7.7 was developed in PowerPoint, using Microsoft Office clip art and drawing features.

Some students benefit from a presentation program that offers more structure to develop their digital stories. Figure 7.8 takes James and Tory's RAFT and inserts it into the storybook template from the program Intellipics Studio (Intellitools, Inc.). Using the same RAFT theme, teachers can set up the basic template, entering a choice of backgrounds and pictures appropriate for young children from the program's picture library into pre-set buttons. As the students write their story, they have access to literacy controls, such as text to speech, word prediction, and spell checking. They are able to illustrate their story by clicking on the pre-set pictures from buttons at the bottom of the screen.

FIGURE 7.8

RAFT Writing Using a Template from Intellipics Studio®

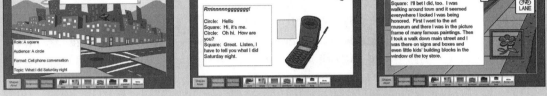

Source: Diagram created using Classroom Suite® by Intellitools, Inc. Used with the permission of Intellitools, Inc.

Mr. Cooper may take further advantage of the RAFTing strategy by forming groups of four students to create story problems based on the RAFTs. Using the RAFT about rectangles, the first student in one of the groups wrote the first sentence of the problem: "On an evening walk I came upon a sign with two sets of parallel lines." The second student picked up the story problem by writing: "The parallel lines also looked like they were the same length." The third student added: "To be sure I pulled out my T-ruler and compass, and sure enough both sets of lines were parallel and all four lines were the same length. What shape was it?" The fourth and final student of the group had to answer the question in the final line of the story problem: "The sign was in the shape of a rectangle called a square." Mr. Cooper had the other group members verify the answer and discuss the problem as a group to make any necessary revisions. Groups then exchanged their story problems for further practice in applying new understandings.

TIPS

Wilkinson (2001) offers the following tips for developing digital stories for math:

- Keep length short (5–15 frames is sufficient).
- Keep text short and images simple.

- Use audio capability as needed (e.g., provide button for non-readers to have book read to them).

- Include page forward and back options (to allow reader to "flip" pages back and forth).

- Maintain a story line.

- Save in read-only format.

- If students are creating their own, give them a basic format and include a rubric.

- Be aware of copyright issues and the possibility of infringement.

- Use consistent background and text fonts as appropriate.

- Use a clip art file appropriate for young children.

- Encourage students to create their own designs and images using a digital camera or drawing software. (p. 60)

Looking Back

As you discovered, Mr. Cooper's math class enjoyed the benefits of his imaginative applications of technology-mediated content literacy strategies for learning geometry terms and concepts. Mr. Cooper presented lesson impressions, word grids, and RAFT writing in ways that stimulated students from all ability levels to respond actively, generate meaningful ideas, and reflect on new understandings. Mr. Cooper knew that he could sustain the students' attention to learning by giving them opportunities to interact with geometry content using digital formats at each phase of the lesson. You also learned that commonly available software can be versatile tools in the hands of content teachers. Be sure to reflect on the multiple applications of technology by the teachers showcased in Chapters 4, 5, 6, and 7, and consider how the various technology tools can serve your own strategic content teaching.

Questions for Study

- Which technology applications and content literacy strategies employed by Mr. Cooper can you and your colleagues most readily put to use in teaching lessons from your own curriculum?

Think about how this could be accomplished with a specific topic, a specific literacy strategy, and a specific technology application.

- Among the descriptions and references to multimedia made in this chapter, which would you like to learn more about? In your role as a literacy coach, classroom teacher, or administrator, establish and/or participate in a team that gathers useful information about and skills with this software?

References

NCTM. (2000). *Standards for school mathematics*. Accessed on June 12, 2007, from http://standards.nctm.org/document/chapter3/comm.htm

Silbey, R. (2003, April). Math out loud! *Instructor, 7,* 112.

Wilkerson, T. (2001). Reading and writing the digital way: Using digital books to teach math. *Learning and Leading with Technology, 29*(3) 42–45, 60–61.

Resources

General:
- National library of virtual manipulatives: http://nlvm.usu.edu/en/nav/vlibrary.html
- Video clips: www.unitedstreaming.com/
- Digital Storyteller, a Web-based tool to construct narratives: www.digitalstoryteller.org/
- Classroomclipart.com
- Fusion: www.writerlearning.com/
- Free source of pictures for noncommercial purposes: Flickr (www.flickr.com)
- English/Spanish translation of math terms: www.math.com/tables/spanish/eng-spa.htm

Safe blogging for classrooms:
- The Blog-Meister, created by educator and speaker David Warlick: http://classblogmeister.com
- Blogspot: www.blogspot.com
- E-pals: www.epals.com
- IMBEE: www.imbee.com/
- Center for Technology and Teacher Education's blogging activities page: www.teacherlink.org/content/blog

Technology Tools for Content Literacy Support

Seeing Forward

What follows is a review of the technology tools that have been used throughout this book. In this review, we highlight particular features that we have found useful in literacy development. We invite you to skip around in this section, lingering on discussions that perhaps reveal hidden features or strategies that you had not considered, or skimming areas where you have had considerable experience.

You will notice in this discussion that many of software programs and vendors are mentioned by name. This is meant to illustrate or to provide examples of the types of products that we are describing. We do not officially endorse any of these products or vendors, nor do we have a business relationship with any of these companies. An annotated list at the end of this chapter provides a reference point for further information.

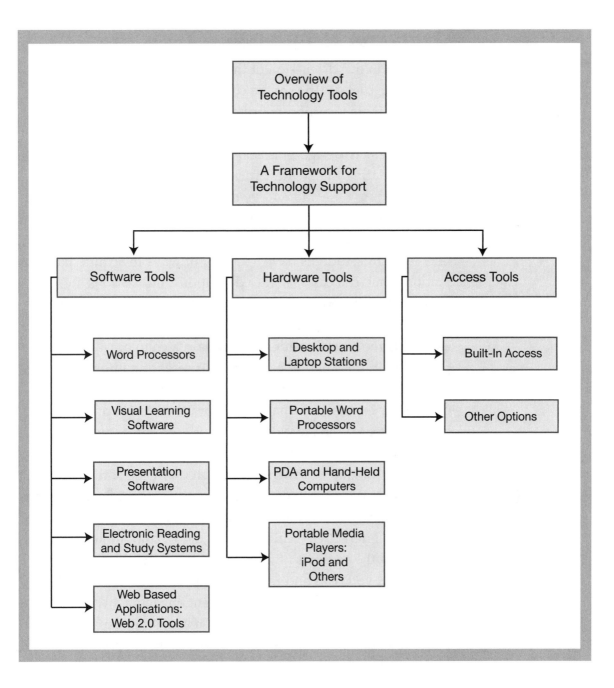

Overview of Technology Tools

As we begin our discussion of the technology tools used to support literacy, let us first set the context by considering the ways that these tools incorporate principles of Universal Design for Learning (UDL). Recall from the discussion in earlier chapters that universally designed lessons give teachers flexibility in accommodating the greatest variety of learning needs, rather than spending time and energy developing adaptations after the fact (Rose & Meyer, 2002). The first principle of UDL is to present concepts in multiple formats. When technology is used to present new learning, students have a variety of ways to acquire information. They can easily link to definitions, translations, models of possible solutions, or websites with background information. A concept can be supported using voice, images, music, video, as well as the text. Consider how certain technology applications presented in this chapter can support presenting information in multiple formats. Technology can also give students multiple options for expressing what they know, the second principle of UDL. Students who have difficulty with written expression can benefit from being able to talk about it, and to illustrate their learning with either drawings or graphics. Many of the technology applications presented in this chapter support flexible means of student expression. Finally, creative use of technology can encourage interactivity, collaboration, and exploration of interests far beyond the confines of the printed page, the third principle of UDL. As you read and review the applications presented here, consider how they can promote student engagement and motivation. Support in these three areas of presentation, expression, and engagement will help to develop academic literacy—the reading, writing, speaking, listening, and viewing skills needed for most school-based tasks (Brozo & Simpson, 2007).

Although technology can provide timely and independent support for reading (Edyburn, 2003), merely using these tools does not automatically mean the student will learn the material

(Boone & Higgins, 2005). Struggling readers may not be able to successfully utilize reading supports without proper instruction, and may need to be shown how to make sense of material that is complex (Strangman & Dalton, 2005). Consult earlier chapters for examples on how content literacy strategies can be paired with these technology tools.

A Framework for Technology Support

Our framework for technology support centers around three sets of tools: software, hardware, and access tools commonly available in most classrooms. The first set of tools is software applications. We highlight useful features and supports available in four common types of software programs: word processors, visual learning software, presentation programs, and electronic reading and study programs. In reviewing each type of software program, we begin with the most common features, and then look at further supports or adjustments that are available for your students. Web-based applications, accessible with an Internet connection and a browser, are also included. The second set of tools is hardware. We offer suggestions for maximizing your use of available computer hardware resources, and for looking at lower-cost alternatives and emerging trends. The third set of tools is access technology. Many adjustments for students with physical challenges in vision, hearing, or movement are built in to the operating system of the computer. These adjustments are reviewed, and we offer suggestions obtaining additional support if needed.

Software Tools

First, let's clarify the type of software we will be featuring. Most of us realize that software is needed in order for us to operate a computer as intended. When we describe software programs typically found in schools, we usually are talking about three distinct categories: operating system, educational, and application.

Operating system software provides the master control for the computer. Personal computer (PC) platforms typically use Microsoft Windows (XP or Vista) software, and Apple computers use Mac OS (usually X or above). A third option, Linux, is used in a few school districts. It is a free, open source operating system that is popular with programmers and software developers. It is important to know which operating system the computer is using, since each system has its own set of commands and will sometimes only operate certain other types of software. In this chapter we will be describing software programs that work using either Windows or Mac operating systems, and may occasionally describe commands that work on one platform or the other. We will look at some of the features built in to operating system software during the discussion of access tools.

Educational software is designed to assist in the teaching-learning process. Usually, educational software includes the content or skills that will be taught. Examples are numerous in schools; this type of software includes drill and practice, tutorials, and educational simulations and games. Although educational software can be useful to teach concepts and to motivate students, it is not the focus of this book.

Our focus is on *application software*—the software that can be used to produce a letter, to write an essay, or to develop a presentation. There are numerous types of application software, such as databases, spreadsheets, and desktop publishing programs, but we will concentrate on four types most commonly found in K–12 environments and can be used as tools to support the development of literacy. These are word processors, visual learning software, presentation software, and electronic reading and study systems. This section explores useful features within each of these software types. We encourage you to use these software tools as often as possible and on a routine basis, and to be aware of specialized software for students who need additional support.

Word Processors

Most of us are quite familiar with word-processing programs, and we encourage their use throughout the writing process. Beyond the process of entering text and editing for errors in spelling and grammar, we have found the following features to be most useful when used as literacy supports. This discussion is based on *Microsoft Word 2007*.

Basic Formatting Skills

Sometimes students (and also, perhaps, their teachers) will use the space bar or tabs instead of formatting tools to move text to the center or right side of the line, or try to put a "carriage return" (an old typewriting term, replaced by the enter key on computers) at the end of each line. This then causes alignment problems when editing, changing the font size, or printing the text. Although most teachers and students know and use basic text formatting features, an explanation of their use still bears repeating.

Remind students that word processors "wrap" each line automatically. The enter key is used only to designate the start of a new paragraph, not the start of a new line. Knowing how to change the horizontal alignment of a document is also important. Sometimes students will tab or space over to the perceived center of the screen instead of using the centering alignment, or tab or space to make the edge text flush with the right margin instead of using the right alignment button. Alignment tools are usually located as buttons on the toolbar. Encourage students to look for formatting errors; all formatting marks can be viewed through the tools>options settings of most word processors.

Spell and Grammar Check

Spell and grammar check are invaluable tools for most writers. This feature, when turned on, tags errors: a red underline for a misspelled word, and a green underline for words, phrases, or punctuation that do not conform to standard grammar rules.

Clicking on the red notice (or right click using a PC) will produce a dialog box of suggested spelling corrections that can be selected. Clicking anywhere in the green (grammar) notice produces a dialog box that states the rule, suggests options, and offers an explanation of the rule. Students may be encouraged to use these features in several ways, as they type or compose their work, during the editing process, and during a final revision.

This feature may be turned off in the tools > options section of most word processors. Students may then use the word processor to take a spelling test, to compose answers to essay questions, or in other forms of writing assessment in which access to spelling or grammar aids would prevent the measurement of a targeted skill (Castellani & Jeffs, 2001).

Reference Tools: Look Up, Synonyms, Thesaurus, Translate

These reference tools are invaluable aids to the writing process for everyone. Show the students how to click on the word in question (right click on Windows, single click on Mac) to access a dialog box. Scroll down the options for obtaining a definition, getting a list of synonyms, accessing the thesaurus, and translating the word. Some of these features are stored within the word-processing program; others may require an Internet connection in order to access.

Tables

Use tables to organize information in a format that will retain its shape when new information is added. The tables feature is preferable to using tabs when displaying information in lists of two or more columns. Tables can be created in a variety of formats, borders, and shadings. The tables feature is useful for displaying and discussing several content area literacy strategies, such as critical features and KWL charts.

Diagrams and Drawing Tools

Opening the drawing tools on the toolbar displays a variety of shapes that can be used to make diagrams and concept maps.

Most word processors also offer a number of pre-formatted diagrams that can be inserted into a document.

Document Templates

Templates save document text and settings in a format that can be modified or added to without changing the original. Document templates are used to automate the process of composing reports that display information in a standard format, such as legal documents, psychological reports, and medical reports. Templates are also used in business applications, such as letters and fax coversheets. When a template is open, the document that appears on the screen is given a different name form the original (such as Document 1). Once the new information is typed into this document, it is saved as a regular document with a different name, leaving the original intact. Most word-processing programs offer multiple examples of ready-made document template formats.

For classroom use, saving quizzes, exams, and report formats as document templates allows for multiple uses of that document without changing the original. For example, a simple fill-in-the blank quiz, saved as a template, will open on a student computer with the file name Document 1 (or a higher number). The student may then take the test using the word processor. The only option for saving the document asks for a new document name (save as), keeping the original blank test intact for another student to use.

Document templates are also useful tools for structuring the writing process for students. Some students have great difficulty expressing their knowledge in written formats. When the learning task involves communicating summaries or results, consider devising a template to use as a guide. Make generic statements in a word-processing document, with spaces or blanks for the student to add specific information. A book report format, for example, could be saved as a document template with a descriptive name, such as "nonfiction book report." When the document reopens, the student provides the "save as" name (such as "Mary's book report"), leaving the original document intact.

Readability

Word-processing programs automate the task of checking the readability level of a selection. Obtain a sample of the text by typing a sample selection, usually 100 words or more, into a document (or by cutting and pasting a digital version obtained from the Internet, by scanning, or other methods). In Microsoft Word 2007, set the spelling and grammar check functions (tools>options>spelling and grammar tab) to check readability statistics. A readability score is provided after the spelling and grammar check is run from the tools menu. The readability level of a text can help teachers select reading material that is within the ability level of the student.

Auto Summarize

The auto summarize feature identifies the key points based on the frequency of words used within the document. The user chooses a percentage of sentences containing these higher-frequency words to display in a summary, and can select the manner in which this summary is displayed—highlight key points, insert an abstract at the top of a document, or view only the summary. The percentage of sentences displayed from the original document can be increased or decreased from a slider bar. The auto summarize feature gives the best results when used on documents with a predictable structure, such as textbooks and articles. It does not produce as satisfactory a summary for selections without a predictable structure, such as works of fiction.

Auto summarize has been used with struggling readers as a metacognitive strategy. Students can evaluate their own need for the amount of information, given the learning task at hand. It can also be used for motivation, allowing students to choose the amount of text and detail that they are willing to read initially, or as a prereading strategy, showing key points in order to elicit questions or activate background knowledge discussions (Edyburn, 2002).

Settings to Improve Access for Students with Physical Challenges

The default settings on word processors can be changed to accommodate visual and motor needs of many students. Experiment with the following features to determine if you or your students find them useful.

- *Zoom box.* The zoom box can be used to increase the size of the screen display without increasing the font size of the printed text. The zoom option is located on the toolbar and/or in the view menu. This feature makes reading the text on the screen more comfortable for students with visual challenges. It is also a useful for adults experiencing eyestrain or the inevitable near-vision challenges of middle age.

- *Text color and background color.* Try changing the color of the text, or the color of the background, using the format menu. This feature can provide greater contrast between the foreground and background for students with visual challenges, or can simply be used to add motivation and interest. Experiment with a variety of settings here. Black text on yellow background provides high contrast. Two contrasting colors that are soothing are dark blue text on a gray background.

- *Speech recognition.* Speech recognition allows numbers and words to be verbally dictated directly into a word processor. It is accurate enough to be a useful tool for students who have difficulty expressing their thoughts in written format, or for students and teachers with movement challenges, such as fatigue or difficulty in typing. The speech recognition feature must first be activated by training the program to recognize a particular voice by reading prepared text from a set-up screen. A high-quality headset microphone, in a consistent position about an inch to the side of the mouth, and a quiet room will increase recognition accuracy. The accuracy level of speech recognition is expected to improve with scheduled upgrades of Microsoft products. The speech recognition feature included with most word processors does not support a totally hands-free operation, however. It still requires use of the keyboard for corrections and for some commands. Students who need completely hands-free operation should use a software program designed specifically for speech recognition, such as *Dragon Naturally Speaking.* This program comes in versions customized for the type of vocabulary that will be used, and is now voice independent, meaning that it can recognize most words without the need to train the voice or use specialized microphones. Expect this exciting technology feature to improve with subsequent upgrades.

Specialized Word-Processing Features

Specialized word processors offer features that are not currently available in typical office-based applications, or are specially designed for use in K–12 environments. These specialized features offer additional support for students who struggle with academic literacy skills.

Text to speech (*TTS* or "talking word processors") reads or narrates the text displayed in the document. Some of these programs merely read the selected text. Others highlight the text as it is read, increasing the visual prompt for the student. Text-to-speech word processors support reading, writing and spelling for emerging readers or struggling students.

Two text-to-speech word processors developed for K–12 use are Intellitalk (Intellitools, Inc.) and Write: Outloud (Don Johnston, Inc.). Both of these products highlight words as read, providing a bimodal approach to the screen—visual as well as auditory—that some students need in order to make progress in their reading. These programs also offer a choice of reading voices and speed, text-to-speech spell checking, dictionary and thesaurus support, a large picture library, and a choice of very simple word-processor picture commands for younger students. Both programs have extensive collections of picture libraries, templates, and activities for instructional support.

Other text-to-speech options are included (free) as operating system software features. On Mac platforms, Simple Text is available on version 7.5 and higher, and Voice Over is available on Mac OS X (Tiger and the upgrade Leopard). These built-in features will read the text in a word-processing document.

In Windows XP, Narrator announces keystrokes and sections of text in a document. The speech toolbar of Microsoft Office (tools>speech) has a speak text function. It will read text aloud from the point of cursor entry until the stop command is pressed. Try these options out with your students to determine if they are appropriate. Most of these built-in or low-cost features do not highlight text as it is read. Some students may benefit from the word highlighting feature and the convenience of other controls found in a program designed for classroom use.

A quick Internet search results in several sites where free or donation text-to-speech programs may be downloaded. Two programs in particular have received good reviews from users. ReadPlease offers a free version of text-to-speech software as well as an upgraded version at a modest price (www.readplease.com/). Sayz Me (www.datafurnace.net.au/sayzme/html/home.html) is a free program specifically for the Windows platform. In both of these programs, the reading is not automatic. Text must be pasted from a document into the program in order to activate the TTS feature. Free software can seem like a great alternative for schools with tight technology budgets. However, be sure to check with the technology coordinator before downloading any program from the Internet. Because some programs can potentially conflict with network and other settings, districts usually have policies governing this practice.

Word Prediction

Word prediction suggests a list of intended words from the first few keystrokes and presents the user with choices that can be inserted with one keystroke or mouse click. Predictions are based on spelling, word frequency, and syntax. Most word predication programs include text-to-speech options that read intended choices aloud. Originally intended for users with physical disabilities, this feature has been recommended for students with difficulties in transcription, word retrieval, spelling, and fine-motor skills (MacArthur, 1998).

Word prediction can be a feature within a specialized word processor. Intellitalk is an example of a specialized word processor with this feature. Other word prediction programs work as a support to standard word processors. Examples of this type of program are Read and Write Gold (textHelp, Inc.) and Co: Writer (Don Johnston, Inc.). These programs operate as a toolbar that opens a word prediction window within programs such as Microsoft Word or Write: OutLoud.

Many software programs with word prediction are available in 30-day product demonstration versions, either as a download or on CD-ROM. Factors to consider when choosing a word predication program include ease of use for the student, the sophistication level of the vocabulary it is possible to predict, and the ability to add additional words.

Rebus Word Processor

A rebus is a picture or symbol that is used in place of or to describe a written word. Rebus reading programs have been used with emerging readers, English language learners, or students with severe reading difficulties (Edyburn, 2002). Rebus word processors automatically insert a picture above an individual word. Most have picture dictionaries of several thousand words and have text-to-speech features. Examples of rebus-based word processors are Picture It, PixWriter, and Writing with Symbols.

Visual Learning Software

Visual learning strategies have long been recommended to assist students in text comprehension and in study skills. These strategies are called a variety of names—idea maps, concept maps, story boards, advanced organizers, webs, and semantic maps. They help students organize ideas during reading and writing, understand the structure and content of the text, take notes in an organized manner, and in vocabulary development (Bulgren, Schumaker, & Deschler, 1988; Gardill & Jitendra, 1999).

Teachers and students have typically used visual learning strategies by drawing a diagram by hand. This method has its advantages. A hand-drawn diagram can be spontaneous and is low-tech. But software applications can also be used to produce visual maps. Using visual learning software brings the advantages of working in a digital environment to these powerful strategies. In a digital environment, the display can be quickly changed in appearance or in format (for example, increasing the size of the screen or having the text read aloud). Students can access other areas for additional information, using hyperlinks to explanatory files or websites. Using visual learning software programs in this manner gives teachers curriculum flexibility. Teachers can build in options that support learning differences from the beginning, reducing the need to modify or create alternate assignments or adapt for special learners after the fact (Rose & Meyer, 2002). Visual learning software has been effective when used with diverse learners in general education settings (Anderson-Inman, Knox-Quinn, & Horney, 1996). Other studies pair the use of visual learning software with content area literacy strategies (Puckett & Brozo, 2005).

There are several options for visual learning software, but most classrooms use Inspiration or Kidspiration (Inspiration Software, Inc.). Inspiration is suitable for upper elementary, secondary, or adult students. Kidspiration is a simplified version of the same program, and is more suitable for grades K–5. These programs open in a diagram view. This view has three sets of controls: a symbol pallet, which is a collection of shapes and pictures organized around themes; a diagram toolbar for showing relationships between the various symbols; and a formatting toolbar to control font options and symbol colors. Using this view, teachers and students can use brainstorming as a group technique, generating ideas together and later using linking tools between concepts to illustrate relationships. Students can also use the program to create webs, diagrams, or maps to organize and analyze information. Both versions provide extensive templates, which can be used or modified when a particular type of diagram, such as a Venn diagram or a character web, is desired. While the students work in the diagram view, the program is generating an outline of the work in the background, with the text organized according to the topics and subtopics indicated by links developed in the diagram view. Students may enter text and notes into this outline and export it to a word-processing program. The Inspiration website (www.inspiration.com) provides additional suggestions for visual learning strategies, sample lesson plans, and links to curriculum integration literature.

A lower-cost option for visual learning software is to use the diagram and drawing features of a word processor. Although the drawing and diagram features are not as easy to use and do not automatically generate an outline, they are a readily available alternative.

Specialized Visual Learning Software

Specialized visual learning software offers features that give additional support for students who struggle with academic literacy skills.

Draft:Builder (available from Don Johnston, Inc., www .donjohnston.com) is a structured visual learning software program that emphasizes planning, organizing, and draft writing strategies. An extensive list of templates guides the student through the writing process in a variety of subject areas. The structured nature of Draft:Builder makes it especially suitable for students with special needs or for those who have a need for more sophisticated technology support in writing. Draft:Builder interfaces with other reading and writing supports (text-to-speech word processing, word prediction) offered in a SOLO, a suite of products by the same company.

Presentation Software

Presentation software allows teachers and students to use more than one type of media—text, graphics, audio, animation, and/or video—to communicate a message. For students who are living in today's technology-rich environment, these multimedia combinations get and hold students' attention and can increase the learning and motivation of learners (O'Bannon and Puckett, 2007; Moore, Burton, and Myers, 2004).

Presentation programs are quite simple to use and are readily available in most classrooms. They all have similar basic operations. A screen, or page, is displayed, and the user adds color, text, graphics, audio, or video to this page. Subsequent pages with a choice of additions are then created and modified as needed. Page formats—such as titles, text size, background, and color—can be saved as templates. The user can specify the order in which the pages are displayed (linear—one after the other, or nonlinear—with links to internal or external pages or sites). Once the file is completed, it is played as a slide show that can be shown on individual computer screens or projected to a larger group.

PowerPoint (Windows/Mac) and Keynote (Mac only) are the most widely available of these presentation software products. Other software programs that were developed specifically for use in K–12 environments include Kid Pix Deluxe, HyperStudio, and Intellipics Studio. These software programs feature a variety of templates for developing multimedia activities. Examples offered by the various vendors include templates for book reports, writing prompts, adaptive books, quizzes, math activities, spelling practice, and basic phonics activities. Teachers and students add their own content to the template examples. Intellipics Studio also has built-in features that allow a student with physical challenges to access the program using a single switch or a programmable keyboard. Finally, the program Kerpoof (www.kerpoof. com) is a free, online multimedia program designed for use in K–8 environments. The program and files created with it can be accessed and shared from any computer with an Internet connection, making it ideal for collaborative and home-school projects.

Two widely available video editing and presentation programs are Movie Maker (Windows) and iMovie (Mac). These programs are either automatically preloaded along with the computer's system software, or are available through download. Accompanying instructions and tutorials give clear guidance on using these programs. Movie Maker and iMovie are used to edit video segments when only a portion of the original clip is needed. The edited clips can then be combined with other video clips, additional audio tracks, and text to make a stand-alone movie. These clips can also be inserted into presentation programs, such as PowerPoint.

The ways that teachers and students may use presentation software in learning is only limited by the imagination of the user. Teachers have used multimedia presentations to develop virtual tours as pre- and postteaching activities for field trips or literature study, to create tutorials, to accompany demonstrations or discussions, or to document change over time. Students have used presentation tools to construct and express their learning through illustrations, diagrams, summarizing, videos, and recording. They have developed multimedia slide shows to accompany reports, and have documented their progress through portfolios. Presentation programs can be use to promote active learning strategies and increased student engagement. Students can be grouped for whole group, small group collaborative work, and team-building skills. Most researchers agree that teachers should get the students actively involved as quickly as they are developmentally capable of using these tools (O'Bannon & Puckett, 2007).

Electronic Reading and Study Systems

Teachers have always used auditory strategies, such as reading partners or tape-recorded passages, to help students gain access to the content of books. These strategies are useful for anyone who reads slowly, has difficulty recognizing certain words, or has low vision. Indeed, we have seen an increase in popularity of other forms of auditory "text," for the general population, who access books on tape, CD-ROMs, electronic calendars, or iPod (Pierce, 2006).

Although auditory-only strategies make the content of the text available, they are passive systems; listening is the only response needed. Electronic reading and study systems provide interactive, as well as auditory and visual, accommodations for students. They support the use and development of strategies for reading comprehension. The basic core of these programs is to use text-to-speech technology to read what appears on a computer screen. Going beyond screen reading, however, they also have features that support comprehension strategies, such as highlighting, note taking, book marking, and electronic reference. Many also include optical character recognition (OCR) programs that work with a scanner to convert paper-based text to a digital format. These programs are easy to learn, easy to use, and allow the student to obtain needed literacy supports independently.

Obtaining a digitized text source is the key to using this technology support. If the original source is a paper-based textbook, the options are limited to two: retyping the text (a choice that does not help to increase learner independence and is tedious at best) or scanning using optical character recognition software. If one were to scan a page of text using the same software program used to scan a picture, the result is just a graphic of the text. It cannot be read or edited. However, scanning the text using OCR software converts the scanned image into digital text which then operates in a similar manner to text in a word processor. Text-to-speech software can then "read" the digital text, using a choice of voices, rate, and inflections. The easiest way to convert a printed textbook page into a digital version is to use a scanner with software that uses both optical character recognition and text-to-speech programs.

In today's electronic world, scanning large amounts of text in order to convert it to a digital format is a tedious activity. Electronic reading and study systems are easier to use when the source is already in a digital format. Files from the Internet, both text and PDF formats, are readable by most of these systems. Similarly, textbook publishers are beginning to provide classroom materials that are available in digital as well as print format. Most have agreed to follow the National Instructional Materials Accessibility Standards (NIMAS), a set of guidelines for the development of commercially produced digital formats that can be easily transformed to suit the needs of students with print disabilities (CAST, 2006). Recent legislation (IDEA 2004) enables school districts to purchase core K–12 curriculum materials in this format. What this means for teachers and students is that school districts may purchase print as well as electronic versions of adopted texts. These electronic versions are not student-ready, but can be accessed with most electronic reading software. Once accessed through this software, the output can be changed to the dual modalities of spoken word and highlighted text, to an auditory only file (MP3 or WAV), or even to Braille. Expect electronic versions of textbooks to become more widely available for classroom use as states implement this legislation.

A variety of these electronic reading and study systems are available and new products are continuously being developed. The price is related to its ease of use and included features. Some have built-in scanning and conversion software (OCR), and others rely on the publisher to provide an electronic format. Some have the option to convert text to an audio file (such as an MP3 or MP4 format) for audio playback on a portable device (think iPod here). Others have sophisticated literacy supports, such as highlighting, extraction, dictionary, reference, note taking, word processing, and translation capabilities. The following electronic reading and study systems have most of the essential features that struggling readers find useful. Each system has a good track record for classrooms use and can be used by students with a wide variety of needs.

The Kurzweil 3000 (Kurzweil Educational Systems) is an electronic reading and study system with an extensive array of literacy, study, and test-taking supports. The professional version features a built-in OCR that discerns between pictures and text effortlessly, requiring little adjustment from the user. Read-only versions (Learn station) have all the features of the professional version, except for the OCR software. This version reads files converted by the professional version and is offered at a reduced cost.

WYNN (Freedom Scientific Inc.), also frequently purchased for classroom use, features versions with built-in OCR software (WYNN Wizard) as well as read-only versions (WYNN Reader). This program also features an array of literacy and study supports. The text can be viewed as it appears on the page or the size and spacing can be customized according to visual preferences. WYNN has simplified toolbars that can be modified for individual use. The company, Freedom Scientific, Inc., also offers software and hardware products for students who are blind or who have low vision.

Read and Write Gold (textHELP, Inc.) is a program that works in conjunction with standard Windows applications. It has a toolbar that floats (or can be docked) on the screen. It's most popular use is in conjunction with Microsoft Office products (MSWord, Excel, and PowerPoint) for literacy support. Its features include OCR, TTS, and reference support.

Other electronic reading systems commonly found in schools include the AspireReader (Aeguus Technologies Corporation). This software product reads digitized text (TTS) and provides reading and writing supports, but does not have an OCR feature. Premier Assistive Technology (www.readingmadeez.com) has a number of products that are sold only to schools and other organizations. Organizations may choose electronic reading and study features by product, depending on the needs of the users. This company also has a grant program for school districts.

For smaller jobs or for occasional literacy support, the Info Scan (WizCom Technologies) is a hand-held scanner with built-in OCR software. This device is lightweight, reasonable in cost, and ideal for library research. The size of a pen, the Info Scan scans words, directly from the printed page, that can be read, translated, and/or defined. The scanned text may be transferred to word-processing programs on a computer or a PDA.

When digitizing copyrighted material, teachers must be aware of regulations that either permit or restrict the use of this technology. The Chafee Amendment (part of the 1996 amendments to the Copyright Act, Section 121) permits teachers to digitize printed text materials in order to provide a version that is accessible for students with print disabilities. Further reproduction or distribution of these materials, however, is not allowed (NLS, 1996). As currently interpreted, teachers and schools are in compliance with this amendment if the material is used on an individual basis with individuals who are print disabled (Strangman, Hall, & Meyer, 2004; Stahl, 2004). As with most legislation, implementation issues have raised ambiguities and debates. Hopefully, obtaining digital versions from the publishers, bypassing the need to convert to an alternate format, will resolve many of these potential conflicts.

Web-Based Applications

Web-based applications, also known as the *Web 2.0,* are emerging as useful literacy development tools. These applications are usually written using "open source" code that is available from anywhere via an Internet connection, meaning that the software does not have to be loaded on or purchased for a particular machine. These tools are designed so that multiple users can view, collaborate, and revise a shared body of work. Blogs, wikis, and podcasts are the most common examples of these applications for use in classrooms (Soloman & Schrum, 2007).

Blogs

A Web log, shortened to *blog,* is a set of commentaries on a particular topic. The author, or owner, of the blog posts content (in text, images, or hyperlinks), and invites public commentary. Most of the time, the content is displayed in reverse chronological order—newest on top. Blogs are a great way for students to express themselves, improve their writing skills, share what they know, and learn from others. Two suggested blogging tools that are suitable for classroom use are Blogger (www.blogger.com) and Class Blogmeister (http://classblogmeister.com). These tools offer security features—for example, teacher supervision of postings and private "membership"—that may allay concerns of posting student work and inviting public comment. Those who have used blogs in the classroom recommend that you start with small projects, posting assignments or links and inviting comment, to get familiar with the software (Solomon & Schrum, 2007; Richardson, 2006).

Wiki

A *wiki* is a webpage containing content that may be edited or changed by other users. Wikis can be used to obtain information about a topic, but they also function as an online tool for writing, editing, collaborating, or changing the document. Because a wiki is web-based and can be accessed from any computer with an Internet connection, it is an ideal tool for developing collaborative writing groups that could work from school as well as from home. Classrooms, schools, or districts can set up their own wikis that are password protected and secure—meaning that a teacher or designee can approve who can view or edit the pages. Some wiki options include Wikispaces (www.wikispaces.com), which offers space to teachers and has links to ideas for using wikis in education, and MediaWiki (http://mediawiki.org), which is a free, server-based wiki software package.

Podcasting

Podcasting is a term coined in 2004 that combines the words *iPod* and *broadcasting* to mean an audio or video recording available on the Internet that can be downloaded to a portable digital player (Wikipedia, 2006). Although a podcast does not require that one use either an iPod or radio broadcast equipment to develop it, the name has held. Podcasts require a software program, such as *iTunes* (a free download from www.apple.com) to view on a standard desktop or laptop computer. Anyone can develop a podcast using a microphone, a computer with access to the Internet, and free downloadable open-source software for recording and editing sounds (Audacity or Garage Band).

Individuals may subscribe to a podcast site that uses RSS feeds to automatically update web-based material. The initials RSS refer to a file format, such as Really Simple Syndication, or RSS 2.0, that "pushes" any updated content from several webites to one place. Teachers could post lectures, notes, assignments, and presentations to this podcast site, enabling students to conveniently receive the latest or updated information on their portable media devices (such as an iPod) to take with them anywhere. Students can also use the same procedures to develop and post their own podcasts as a way of demonstrating or explaining material learned (Baugh, 2005).

Hardware Tools

In order for a student to take advantage of these software innovations that support literacy development, they must have access to the technology—the computer equipment that drives these software tools. Many technology experts advocate that students should have "any time and any where" access to technology, a concept called *1:1 (one-to-one) computing* (Technology and Learning, 2005). Several school districts across the nation have embraced this idea, and many are beginning to share their implementation plans. Other schools struggle to obtain what is termed a "reasonable level" of computer access; one computer for every five students (President's Committee of Advisors on Science and Technology, 1997). Often, the majority of the computers available in the school are placed in labs rather than classrooms, with access limited by schedule. Few teachers and students have access to a "technology-rich" environment, defined as more than

10 computers per classroom or regular lab access of more than twice per week (Norris, Sullivan, Poirot, & Soloway, 2003; Judge, Puckett, & Bell, 2006).

Desktop and Laptop Stations

Perhaps the idea of 1:1 computing is still a long way off for your school. And, what if you are not teaching in a technology-rich environment? How can you use available resources to maximize the technology that you do have available?

First, take a technology inventory. How much access to technology do your students currently have? Where are available computers located: in classrooms, in computer labs, in the library, in mobile laptop carts? Do most students have access to computers at home to supplement, edit, or publish assignments? What is the status of your school's connectivity to the Internet? How else may you use this resource? Does your school have a full-time or part-time technology coordinator? How can this individual assist you—with software, technical assistance, network issues?

Second, consider ways to manage these resources as you plan lessons. Much of the work for a project may be completed away from school computers, or at home. Information from the Internet may be printed out, editing suggestions may be written on printed drafts of work, and concept maps may be filled in from printed templates. Consider student management issues, too, when planning. Avoid situations where students must stand in line to use a computer, as this may cause disruptions. Use a rotation schedule to assure equitable and orderly access. Unless projecting to the entire class or group, use earphones for all programs with sound. To create a sense of responsible computer use, have students sign in with name, date, and time when using the computer (O'Bannon & Puckett, 2007).

If only one computer is available in your classroom, your options are naturally more limited. Try to obtain a good projection system so that the contents of the screen can be visible to both large and small groups of students. Then, consider using the computer to present information, as a demonstration station, or as a learning center for students to work together in groups. This lone computer can also be used as a teacher workstation, to develop materials for some of the activities mentioned in this book.

If you have several computers, try not to place them all in one location. If possible, arrange them in various locations around the room, away from the traffic flow, close to outlets, and away from the glare from windows. Ideally, extra chairs and flat-top desks can be placed near the area to expand the space for project work. The idea here is to encourage student collaboration and to minimize distractions for those not working on the computers (O'Bannon & Puckett, 2007).

Be proactive. Use as many other computer resources available in your school as possible. Maximize your time in the computer lab with the students. Try to schedule the lab as often as possible, and for times when you are able to be there to provide the necessary guidance and instruction. Avoid sending the class to the lab at times when planning or other duties are scheduled. If your school has mobile laptop carts, be sure that you have scheduled them for every time that is available to you.

Technology is considered to be a "moving target"; what was state of the art two years ago may not be so today. As your school develops and revises its technology plan, you may be asked to assist in the selection of new equipment. We encourage you to stay knowledgeable about changes and trends in hardware, operating systems, and software, and to assist in determining what is right for your school. In fact, the International Society for Technology in Education has developed a set of standards for teachers and essential conditions for schools and communities that support your continued development in this area (ISTE, 2002). As you consider new developments in desktop and laptop hardware, we offer a snapshot of three other equipment options that you may consider as supplements or alternatives for your school.

Portable Word Processors

When the students need access to simple programs, like word processing, consider investing in portable word processors. These products are usually around one-forth the cost of traditional computers. They are battery operated, lightweight, and durable. Text can be entered directly into the device, and either sent to a printer or transferred to a computer-based word processor for further formatting. Consult the list located at the end of this chapter for product examples.

Portable word processors do what the name implies: Their capacity is limited to word processing and to smaller-sized programs (such as keyboarding tutors, word prediction, or visual learning software) that may be installed. Some models are even equipped with wireless Internet access capacity. A portable word processor does not have all the glitz of a "real" computer, such as graphics and color. The screen size is much smaller, and the wireless processing speed is slower. However, for schools with limited resources and a mission of making technology available to as many students as possible, these keyboards can fill the bill. And, as Dan Herlihy (2005) remarked when reviewing their use, "Do you need to drive a Hummer just to get milk?"(p. 26). For certain classroom activities, these low-cost tools may be a simpler alternative to desktop access.

Personal Digital Assistants (PDAs) and Hand-Held Computers

These items are a viable option for providing more access to technology for all students. They take up little space, are easy to use, and are relatively low in cost. This technology makes access to computer technology more of a reality in schools with budgetary challenges (Walser, 2004). Many PDA models support standard applications programs, such as word processing, spreadsheets, visual learning software, dictionary and language translation, and ebook readers. Other devices combine multiple higher end features, such as cells phones, Internet access, image capturing, and GPS navigation systems.

Although a few models (most notably those with cell phone capabilities) include a small built-in keyboard, the typical PDA uses a touch screen for interacting with the device. The user taps the screen, usually with a stylus, to select commands and menu choices. Text is entered in one of three ways. The first method of input is through a virtual, or onscreen, keyboard. A stylus is used to tap the desired letters. The second method uses "graffiti," or letter recognition, to input text. Letters are written with the stylus in a specific area of the screen and are then translated into text. This method of text input has some accuracy issues and requires that the user learn a specific style for writing letters. The third method is to attach portable keyboard to the PDA. This keyboard is purchased as an additional accessory and folds or rolls for easy storage. Most schools that use PDAs report purchasing these portable keyboards with each device. The material entered into PDAs can be synchronized, either by a "bluetooth" device or by cable, with other PDAs and with a host computer. This feature increases the flexibility of using hand-held systems in classrooms.

Although PDAs are manufactured by a variety of vendors, Palm Inc. has been the most assertive in outreach to the K–12 education community. The Palm website (www.palm.com/us/education/) lists snapshots of a variety of uses of their PDAs in classrooms across the United States. For example, teachers report using PDAs for assessment, sending the test and receiving results from students' PDAs. They also upload reading material and assignments to individual PDAs. Students use PDAs in cooperative learning settings, each synchronizing their own contributions to a main document. They also use the devices in the writing process, synchronizing between the hand-held device and a computer for idea development using visual learning software, drafting, editing, and publishing. Class notes taken with the PDA can be spell checked and modified as they are written.

Portable Media Players: iPods and Others

The iPod, offered by Apple Inc., is currently the industry leader for portable media players, but other manufacturers, such as Toshiba, Sony, Samsung, and Microsoft, offer similar devices with different model names (Wikipedia, 2007). The term *iPod* is becoming synonymous with portable media players, much like the term *Kleenex* has become the "norm" for disposable facial tissue. Therefore, we will use this term in a figurative manner to describe features of portable medial players in general. This term may equally apply to features of portable media player models offered by other manufacturers.

The iPod is small, lightweight, and simple to operate. Commands are relayed through a touch-sensitive scroll wheel. Audio output is through bud-like earphones, or optional external speakers. Starting with models released in 2003, the iPod is fully compatible with both Mac and Windows platforms. Depending on the particular model, the iPod can play audio files in MP3, MP4, and WAV formats, as well as many audiobook formats. In addition to playing music and storing files, iPods have some PDA-like features. They can display text files and lists of contacts and schedules that can be synchronized with a host computer. Newer generations released since 2005 include video players (Wikipedia, 2006). The most popular use for these devices is to play music and to store files. However, entertainment is not the only use of these devices. Educators are beginning to use these devices to support literacy in a variety of creative ways.

The iPod allows the user to make a real-time recording that may be stored digitally on the device or in a host computer file. These recordings can document reading "running records" for younger students and document progress as a new language is learned. When paired with other companion software, the iPod can be used to develop flash cards for spelling and vocabulary study.

The iPod's recently acquired capacity to view video has perhaps the most potential to influence educational practices.

Apple's *Education Resources* website offers examples of students using the iPod to record interviews, field-based data, and other voice notes. They then combine the audio files with pictures or video clips using iMovie or Movie Maker for later viewing and sharing using the iPod (Apple Computer, Inc., 2006).

A variation on this technology is a device the size of a flash drive that combines an MP3 player a with battery and a USB port. Most students are familiar with these portable USB MP3 players and use them for listening, storing music and files, and then recharging on any computer USB port. *Key to Access* (Premier Assistive Technology) uses this flash drive format to provide a suite of 10 accessibility tools: (1) a text reader for reading emails and webpages; (2) an E-Text Reader that provides electronic reading and study tools (highlight, bookmark, search and extract text); (3) a talking dictionary; (4) a talking word processor; (5) an OCR scanning program; (6) a program for unlocking PDF files into accessible formats; (7) a text-to-audio program that converts digital documents to MP3 format and stores on the player; (8) an on-screen talking calculator; (9) a word prediction program; and (10) a PDF reader with enhanced accessibility features. These programs are not installed on the computer but are accessed from the flash drive, making them portable for the user. *The Key to Access Vpod,* from the same vendor, has a small screen and plays the MP4 video format files.

Access Tools

All computers have accessibility options and adjustments that are built in to operating system software. These adjustments can change the display, magnify the screen, or change how the keyboard operates. They are very useful for students who have physical challenges, temporary or otherwise. Some of these adjustments are also useful for teachers who are beginning to notice the effects of eyestrain or "aging" near-vision abilities.

Built-In Access

On Windows XP machines, these options are found in the control panel and the accessories program. On Windows machines with Vista operating systems released in 2007, these features are consolidated in the *Ease of Access Center*. On Mac OSX machines, they reside in system preferences, in the *Universal Access Panel*. Occasionally these options are disabled by the school or district computer network administrators. If this is the case in your school, contact the appropriate support to make sure that access to these options is restored on computers that will be used by the students who need them. This may involve polite and proactive action on your part, but be assured that these requests are not unreasonable. Documents that list educational technology standards and disability legislation may serve as a backup for the request (ISTE, 2002; IDEA 2004).

Keyboard Adjustments

The keyboard may be adjusted according to user preferences. *Sticky keys* make it possible to use the shift, control, or alternate keys by pressing one key at a time. This setting makes one-handed typing possible. *Filter keys* adjust the acceptance rate of keystrokes and ignore repeated strokes. Younger students or students with motor control difficulties may find this adjustment beneficial. *Toggle key* settings produce a sound to warn the user whenever a lock key is pressed (cap lock, number lock, or scroll lock). Finally, the keyboard may be bypassed completely with the *on-screen keyboard*. Keys are activated by clicking the mouse or by hovering over the selection as seen on the screen. This feature can be particularly useful for students with mild learning disabilities who get lost when changing visual planes (i.e., when gazing between paper, keyboard, and computer screen). Students who have difficulty using the keyboard may also find the on-screen keyboard useful. This feature may also be used to teach students skills needed for text input in PDAs.

Sound Adjustments

Students with hearing impairments may not hear the sounds or warnings that the computer makes. You may add a visual notice for the sounds by using *sound sentry*, which flashes the caption bar, window, or desktop when a sound is produced, or the feature *show sounds*, which displays a caption for the sound.

Mouse Adjustments

Mouse settings use the numeric keypad on the keyboard to move the pointer. The speed of pointer travel can also be set using this setting. On the Windows platform, the right and left mouse buttons may also be reversed; a feature that left-handed users may appreciate. Since the Mac platform uses a mouse with only one button, this control is not necessary.

Display Adjustments

Display adjustments include color and contrast, cursor size and speed, magnification, and screen reading capabilities. *High contrast* displays colors and fonts designed for easy reading. The options give a choice of several high-contrast color combinations to view the screen display. Examples include white text on a black screen, blue text on a grey screen, and a number of other settings. *Cursor options* adjust the blink rate and width of the cursor. The default blink rate, moderate, may be increased or decreased. Cursor width may be changed, widening it from the narrow default setting. These settings are useful for individuals who would otherwise loose sight of the cursor. Preferences can be determined through experimentation with these settings.

The *magnifier* enlarges the section of the screen nearest the cursor, with the standard screen operating in the background for reference. The zoom, or percentage of magnification, may be adjusted by the user. This adjustment is best used on a temporary basis, as it is awkward to use. Additional hardware (such as a larger screen) and software programs offer options for individuals who need a more permanent solution.

The *narrator* reads screen controls and allows the individual to make selections using the arrow, space, tab, enter, and escape keys. It will also announce letters and keystrokes as they are typed on the screen. Students with print disabilities or low vision may find this setting useful. The current version of narrator is not configured conveniently for students who are blind, however. They will prefer to use an additional screen reading program.

The Mac platform (*OS X Tiger* and above) has consolidated these controls into a feature called *VoiceOver.* This feature offers magnification, keyboard controls, and a text-to-speech reader. It will read anything on the screen—commands, word-processing files, and email. It is designed for individuals who are learning disabled or who are blind, and should operate satisfactorily enough to limit the need for expensive add-on screen reading programs.

Speech Recognition

Speech recognition features can be used to control the computer with voice commands. On the Mac, this feature is speaker independent, which means that the user does not have to "train" the voice or use a special microphone. One hundred commands are preprogrammed into the operating system, but the user can develop additional commands. On the Windows platform, this feature requires the user to set up the voice recognition files by initially reading aloud from prepared text. Teachers may need to modify this procedure for students who have word recognition and fluency difficulties by modeling a sentence or two with the microphone muted, then allowing the student to "echo" the reading unmuted.

Other Options

This list of potential computer adjustments may seem confusing to some, especially if there has not been the need to access these feature in a classroom setting before. The important concept here is that using technology increases the probability that all students will be able to participate in the learning experience (Rose & Meyer, 2002). When teachers create a supportive instructional environment that uses technology routinely, it is much easier to use software or equipment that adapts the learning task for an individual with learning or physical challenges.

For students with more involved physical or cognitive challenges, more sophisticated combinations of software and hardware may be necessary. For example, a student whose physical limitations prevent the use of mouse, keyboard, or voice may need to use a single action, such as an eye blink, or a sip and puff from a specialized straw, to control a computer. Although a review of this type of assistive technology is beyond the scope of this book, what is important for classroom teachers to understand is that technology can give these students the access to the same concepts that their peers are learning. Assistive technology services should be available to assist teachers in providing for students with highly specialized needs.

THINK and APPLY

For each of the following categories of software and hardware, visit one vendor website from the URLs provided at the end of this chapter. List as much information as possible from this website that would help you in determining each product's appropriate use in your school or classroom.

Category: Word Processors	Product	Vendor and Website	Demo or trial provided? Y N Cost (range) _____
How this product may be useful in my current classroom situation.			

Category: Specialized Word Processors	Product	Vendor and Website	Demo or trial provided? Y N Cost (range) _____
How this product may be useful in my current classroom situation.			

Category: Visual Learning Software	Product	Vendor and Website	Demo or trial provided? Y N Cost (range) _____
How this product may be useful in my current classroom situation.			

Category: Presentation Software	Product	Vendor and Website	Demo or trial provided? Y N Cost (range) _____
How this product may be useful in my current classroom situation.			

Category: Electronic Reading and Study Systems	Product	Vendor and Website	Demo or trial provided? Y N Cost (range) _____
How this product may be useful in my current classroom situation.			

Category: Portable Word Processors	Product	Vendor and Website	Demo or trial provided? Y N Cost (range) _____
How this product may be useful in my current classroom situation.			

Category: PDAs	Product	Vendor and Website	Demo or trial provided? Y N Cost (range) _____
How this product may be useful in my current classroom situation.			

Category: Computers	Product	Vendor and Website	Demo or trial provided? Y N Cost (range) _____
How this product may be useful in my current classroom situation.			

Category: Presentation and Projection Systems	Product	Vendor and Website	Demo or trial provided? Y N Cost (range) _____
How this product may be useful in my current classroom situation.			

Looking Back

The technology tools described here are readily available or easily purchased for most classrooms and are easy to use. These tools can greatly assist teachers in developing lessons that meet the widest variety of academic needs in the classroom, and lessen the need to adapt lessons for struggling students. What's more, they can be used with effective, evidence-based literacy practices at each phase of a lesson. This chapter can serve as reference when revisiting examples of content literacy strategies paired with technology.

Questions for Study

■ **Play!**

1. In the Think and Apply section, you found that some vendors provide free trial or demonstration versions of their software. Download trial versions of as many of the following as you are able to accomplish in the time allotted: specialized word processor, visual learning software, presentation software, and/or electronic reading and study systems. Explore these programs and determine their suitability for students in a range of grade and content levels.

2. Visit the website Read Write Think (www.readwritethink.org/), a joint effort between IRA and NCTE to promote reading and language arts instruction. This site features interactive online student materials and tools. Follow the student materials link and explore several of the online tools as well as lesson planning suggestions. Critique the suitability of these tools for a range of student levels and needs.

■ **Discuss and Plan**

Individually, or as a group or committee, discuss which of these products or online tools have merit for classroom use. What features of these resources support principles of Universal Design for Learning? How do they support content literacy skills? Identify the most desirable of these products or resources. How can they be implemented in your current teaching situation? What are the barriers to their implementation that would have to be addressed? Where can you find additional information to assist you to incorporate these ideas into current curricular responsibilities?

Product Examples Used in K–12 Classrooms

Prior to ordering any product mentioned here, check the compatibility of the software with the operating system. Older operating systems may not support these products, and conversely, an upgrade in operating system may necessitate and upgrade in software.

Operating System Software

Windows XP, Microsoft Corporation, www.microsoft.com/

Windows Vista, Microsoft Corporation, www.microsoft.com/

Mac OSX Tiger and Leopard, Apple Computer, Inc., www.apple.com/

Linux, Linux Online, Inc., www.linux.org/

Word Processors

Microsoft Office Word 2003, Microsoft Corporation, www.microsoft.com/

Microsoft Office Word 2007, Microsoft Corporation, www.microsoft.com/

Specialized Word Processing Software

Intellitalk III, Intellitools, Inc. (a Cambium Learning Technologies Company), www.intellitools.com/

Write:Outloud, Don Johnston Inc., www.donjohnston.com/

Co:Writer, Don Johnston, Inc, www.donjohnston.com/

Dragon Naturally Speaking, Nuance Communications, Inc., www.nuance.com/

Picture it and Pix Writer, Slater Software, Inc., www.slatersoftware.com/

Writing with Symbols, Mayer Johnson, www.mayer-johnson.com/

Visual Learning Software

Inspiration and Kidspiration, Inspiration Software, Inc., www.inspiration.com

Draft:Builder, Don Johnston, Inc., www.donjohnston.com/

Presentation Software

Microsoft Office PowerPoint 2003, Microsoft Corporation, www.microsoft.com/

Keynote, Apple Computer, Inc., www.apple.com/

Movie Maker, Microsoft Corporation, www.microsoft.com/

iMovie, Apple Computer, Inc. www.apple.com/

Intellipics Studio, Intellitools, Inc., (a Cambium Learning Technologies Company) www.intellitools.com/

Hyperstudio. The Software Mackiev Company. www.mackiev.com/hyperstudio/index.html

Kerpoof, www.kerpoof.com.

Kidpix Deluxe, Broderbund, Inc. www.broderbund.com/

Electronic Reading and Study Systems

AspireReader, Aequus Technologies Corporation, www.aequustechnologies.com

Accessibility Suite and other products, Premier Assistive Technology, www.readingmadeez.com/

Info Scan, WizCom Technologies Ltd., www.wizcomtech.com/

Kurzweil 3000, Kurzweil Educational Systems, Inc. (a Cambium Learning Technologies Company), www.kurzweiledu.com

Read and Write Gold, Texthelp Systems Ltd., www.texthelp.com

WYNN, Freedom Scientific, Inc., www.freedomscientific.com

Portable Word Processors

Neo and Dana, Alpha Smart, Inc., www.alphasmart.com/

QuickPAD, Enablemart, Inc., www.enablemart.com/

The Writer, Advanced Keyboard Technologies, Inc., www.writerlearning.com

Laser PC6, Perfect Solutions Software, Inc., www.perfectsolutions.com

Personal Digital Assistants and Portable Digital Media Players

iPod, Apple Computer, Inc., www.apple.com/

PAC Mate, Freedom Scientific, Inc., www.freedomscientific.com

Tungsten E2 or the Palm TX, Palm, Inc., www.palm.com/us/

Key to Access and Key to Access Vpod, Premier Assistive Technology, Inc., www.readingmadeez.com/

Computers
Windows Computers

Dell, Inc., www.dell.com/

Gateway, Inc., www.gateway.com/index.shtml

Hewlitt-Packard Development Company, L.P., www.hp.com/

Apple Computers

Apple Computer, Inc., www.apple.com/

Presentation and Projection Systems

Information on Projectors and Interactive Whiteboards:

InfoComm International, an international trade association of the professional audiovisual and information communications industries, maintains a list of vendors for a variety of audiovisual products.

Find information on projection systems and interactive whiteboards at this site: http://catalogs.infocommiq.com/

Toolkit Information

Further information on free and vendor-based toolkits has been developed and is regularly maintained by Cheryl Wissick (2007) and is available at www.ed.sc.edu/caw/toolbox.html.

References

Anderson-Inman, L., Knox-Quinn, C., & Horney, M. (1996). Computer-based study strategies for students with learning disabilities: Individual differences associated with adoption level. *Journal of Learning Disabilities, 29,* 461–484.

Apple Computer, Inc. (2006). *Educational resources.* Retrieved August 7, 2006, from www.apple.com/education/solutions/ipod/lessons/index.html.

Baugh, D. (2005). *Classroom uses for iPod and iTunes.* Accessed on August 7, 2006, from http://213.232.94.135/ipodined/e107_files/downloads/ClassroomUsesfor%20iPodandiTunes.pdf.

Boone, R., & Higgins, K. (2005). Designing digital materials for students with disabilities. In D. Edyburn, K. Higgins, & R. Boone (Eds.), *Handbook of special education technology research and practice* (pp. 481–492). Whitefish Bay, WI: Knowledge by Design.

Brozo, W. G., & Simpson, M. L. (2007). *Content literacy for today's adolescents: Honoring diversity and building competence* (5th ed.). Upper Saddle River, NJ: Merrill/Prentice-Hall.

Bulgren, J., Schumaker, J. B., & Deschler, D. (1988). Effectiveness of a concept teaching routine in enhancing the performance of

LD students in secondary-level mainstream classes. *Learning Disability Quarterly, 11*(1), pp. 3–17.

CAST. (2006). *About NIMAS.* Accessed August 15, 2006, from http://nimas.cast.org/about/index.html.

Castellani, J., & Jeffs, T. (May/June 2001). Emerging reading and writing strategies using technology. *Teaching Exceptional Children, 33*(5), 60–67.

Edyburn, D. (2002). Cognitive-rescaling strategies: Interventions that alter the cognitive accessibility of text. *Closing the Gap,* 21(6), 1, 10–11, 21.

Edyburn, D. L. (2003). Rethinking assistive technology. *Special Education Technology Practice, 5*(4), 16–22.

Gardill, M. C., & Jitendra, A. K. (1999). Advanced story map instruction: Effects on the reading comprehension of students with learning disabilities. *The Journal of Special Education, 33*(1), 2–17.

Herlihy, D. (2005). Connect the dots between high incidence disabilities and assistive technology. *Special Education Technology Practice, 7*(5), 23–27.

Individuals with Disabilities Education Act Amendments of 2004. P.L. 108–446.

ISTE. (2002). *National Educational Technology Standards for Teachers.* Eugene OR: International Society for Technology in Education.

Judge, S., Puckett, K., & Bell, S. M. (2006). Closing the digital divide: An update from the Early Childhood Longitudinal Study. *The Journal of Education Research, 100*(1), 52–60.

MacArthur, C. (1998). Word processing with speech synthesis and word prediction: Effects on the dialogue journal writing of students with learning disabilities. *Learning Disability Quarterly, 21*(2), 151–166.

Moore, D. M., Burton, J. K., & Myers, R. L. (2004). Multiple channel communication: The theoretical and research foundations of multimedia. In *Handbook of Research on Educational Communications and Technology* (pp. 981–1008). Mahwah, NJ: Lawrence Erlbaum Associates.

National Library Service for the Blind and Physically Handicapped (NLS). (1996). *NLS Factsheets: Copyright law amendment, 1996: Public Law 104-197.* Accessed on August 13, 2006, from www.loc.gov/nls/reference/factsheets/copyright.html.

Norris, C., Sullivan, T., Poirot, J., & Soloway, E. (2003). No access, no use, no impact: Snapshot surveys of educational technology in K–12. *Journal of Research on Technology in Education, 36*(1), 15–27.

O'Bannon, B., & Puckett, K. (2007). *Preparing to use technology.* Boston: Allyn & Bacon.

Pierce, E. (2006, June). Now hear this: How audible's CEO—himself a published author—is bringing bestsellers and more to your iPod. *Southwest Airlines Spirit*, pp. 88–92.

President's Committee of Advisors on Science and Technology. (1997). *Report to the president on the use of technology to strengthen K–12 education in the United States.* [Online document]. Washington, DC: U.S. Government, Office of Science and Technology Policy. Accessed on August 8, 2006, from www.ostp.gov/PCAST/k-12ed.html.

Puckett, K., & Brozo, W. G. (2005). Using assistive technology to teach content area literacy strategies to students with disabilities. In J. R. Dugan, P. Linder, M. B. Sampson, B. Brancato, & L. Elish-Piper (Eds.), *Celebrating the power of literacy: College Reading Association Yearbook* (pp. 462–479). Commerce, TX: Texas A&M University–Commerce.

Richardson, W. (2006). *Blogs, wikis, podcasts, and other powerful web tools for classrooms.* Thousand Oaks, CA: Corwin Press.

Rose, D., & Meyer, A. (2002). *Teaching every student in the digital age: Universal Design for Learning.* Reston VA: Association for Supervision and Curriculum Development. Accessed on June 22, 2005, from www.cast.org/teachingeverystudent/ideas/tes/.

Solomon, G., & Schrum, L. (2007). *Web 2.0 new tools, new schools.* Eugene OR: International Society for Technology in Education.

Stahl, S. (2004). The promise of accessible textbooks: Increased achievement for all students. *National Center on Accessing the General Curriculum.* Retrieved on August 13, 2006, from www.k8accesscenter.org/training_resources/udl/AccessibletextbooksHTML.asp.

Strangman, N., & Dalton, B. (2005). Technology for struggling readers: A review of the research. In D. Edyburn et al. (Eds.), *The handbook of special education technology research and practice* (pp. 545–569). Whitefish Bay, WI: Knowledge by Design.

Strangman, N., Hall, T., & Meyer, A. (2004) *Background knowledge instruction and the implications for UDL implementation.* National

Center on Accessing the General Curriculum. Retrieved on August 13, 2006, from www.cast.org/publications/ncac/ncac_backknowledgeudl.html.

Technology and Learning. (2005) *1:1 computing: A guidebook to help you make the right decisions*. Accessed on August 8, 2006, from www.techlearning.com/1to1guide/.

Walser, P. (2004). Handheld computers in special education. *Closing the Gap, 23*(2), 1–4.

Wikipedia. (2007). Comparison of portable media players. Retrieved on November 25, 2007, from http://en.wikipedia.org/wiki/Comparison_of_portable_media_players.

Wikipedia. (2006). *Podcasting*. Retrieved on August 7, 2006, from http://en.wikipedia.org/wiki/Podcast.

Wissick, C. (2007). *Web toolboxes: Quickstarts for the web*. Retrieved October 5, 2007, from www.ed.sc.edu/caw/toolbox.html.

Index